Netiquette

DISCARDED

A Comprehensive Guide to Improve, Enhance, and Add Power to Your Email

by
Paul Babicki

This unprecedented how-to book on electronic communications details the rules, practices, and preferred use of language that improves the civility, lucidity, and Netiquette of your email.

ISBN: 1481849522

ISBN 13: 978-1481849524

Library of Congress Control Number: 2012924248
CreateSpace Independent Publishing Platform
North Charleston, South Carolina

Acknowledgments

My foremost acknowledgement goes to my wife, Laurie, who acted as an editor, typist, researcher and designer. Also my deepest thanks go to the late Dr. John C. Fout my dear friend and college advisor who guided me through my academia at Bard College and contributed greatly to my educational foundation. For my business partner, Serkan Gecmen, whose programming skills, brilliant design creations, as shown on this book's cover, and other talents never cease to amaze me. Lastly, I wish to thank my daughters, Anastasia and Alexandra, who always gave me encouragement and support when I needed it.

Table of Contents

Introduction

"I get email; therefore I am."

- Scott Adams

The art and practice of letter writing goes back more than 7,500 years! Civilizations from both the East and West have left many documents to posterity, from the Sumerian ages to Egyptian hieroglyphics to the adages of Confucius through the biblical psalms and epistles up to the Declaration of Independence. More recently, technological advances, such as press and digital printing, have accelerated the speed and delivery of greater amounts of communication.

The first known letter is from 5,000 BC regarding the purchase of a field in the city of UR (Iraq) owned by a person called Annini.

Canberra Times 5/23/1928

The introduction of the Internet has revolutionized not only the speed and delivery of mail but also the very nature of letter writing and communications. Few question the obvious benefits. However, many lament and miss the lack of style, personalization, and ability to impact the experience of communicating to one another. Personal letters have been supplanted by smiley faces, wild blends of fonts, and multimedia attachments. Who can forget a lock of hair, whiff of perfume, or memento included in the contents of a letter or the excitement of seeing a friend or loved one's handwriting on a newly arrived envelope?

Although we cannot yet deliver the personalized qualities through email that letters have provided over the millennia, we can maximize the potential of our electronic correspondences in our personal and professional communications. The intent of this book is to provide all of us who rely on electronic content a means to maximize email's benefits and use the power of our modern language without losing personalized and historical ability to effect change.

Today, email is an integral component of business and personal communications. It's often the vehicle for requesting meetings (business and personal), staying informed at work, or sending prospective employers one's résumé. The list is endless. When people write emails, they want them to be read and responded to. They want action. As with many tasks in life, we all can learn better ways of accomplishing results, and using email etiquette (Netiquette) can dramatically improve the likelihood of getting the desired responses to our emails.

One day, a few years ago, I was in a stationery store picking up supplies for my daughters. Glancing around, I noticed a spiral notebook that had a cover with a matrix of what I presumed was the periodic table of elements. It seemed reasonable that this would be a more educational item than a plain cover, so I purchased several.

Upon arriving home, I was ready to pass the notebooks along when suddenly I noticed that the cover was not what I thought, but rather a matrix of Internet abbreviations for email and texting. This proved to be disconcerting to me and was another example of the way electronic communications is affecting so many aspects of everyday routine and changing emphasis on what were common practices just a few years ago.

This situation is hardly earthmoving, but, among other things, it points to something more troubling. Many facets of education, human interaction, and information are now dependent upon electronic communication and media. Although this has many positive effects, there are many negative ones as well. This brings us to the major catalyst for this book. I have been affected by email in many ways that are discouraging: the proliferation of email, the confusion that can result by misuse, and this list goes on. One of the areas where I felt profound change was email etiquette--Netiquette--compared to letter, phone, and face-to-face etiquette standards of the past. So started the idea for this work. It is intended to reduce the abuse and lack of reasonable standards and to maximize the positive power of email.

Language and vocabulary trends with email

Email has proliferated at a rate few could have foreseen. One hundred forty-four billion (144,000,000,000) emails were sent daily, resulting in more than 52 trillion 560 billion emails in 2012 (Royal Pingdom Tech Blog, January 16, 2013), and the count is growing significantly each year. Despite all of the tools and capabilities technology has contributed to provide better content and communication, proper Netiquette and its requisites have declined as quickly as volume and technology have proliferated. Even more alarming is that a huge number of acronyms, abbreviations, and English (or native language) shortcuts are becoming standardized in even the most formal communications.

Websites, dictionaries, and lists that focus on these new terms are also growing and competing with traditional reference work websites. Seemingly, many users are more interested in learning new acronyms, terms, and phrases. With the lack of standards committees, words are spelled numerous ways, others take on new meaning or characteristics, and still others are alternately presented in upper- and lowercase. Even spell-checkers can be different in their spelling of certain words.

At best, the application of email slang does not help writing in traditional English with correct grammar, structure, or Netiquette. A single error in an email can ruin highly stylized content or a highly structured tone.

Email Netiquette: Why care?

The capabilities technology has given to email and electronic messaging have dynamically changed how people compose, read, and reply to communications. The most obvious of these is the sheer volume of emails sent that is dynamically growing. Many corporate users experienced an average of 112 emails sent and received per day in 2011 (Royal Pingdom), resulting in more than forty thousand emails per year. It is important for a sender to understand that even the opening of an email might be questionable. Once an addressee reads (or scans) the mail, will that person reply? Will the same recipient open a subsequent message? Consciously or not, starting with the inbox, each email user begins to rate the quality (essentially, Netiquette) of each sender. It is, of course, everyone's goal to successfully convey purpose or intent in emails. By consistently employing proper care, consideration, and Netiquette, we can reach this goal.

How many emails are bad?

With the billions of emails being sent every day, 88 to 92 percent of these are abusive (Message Anti-Abuse Working Group, MAAWG). Of those remaining, 50 percent are misunderstood by the recipient, even though 90 percent of the users believe they are sending clear, properly interpreted communications (Nicholas Epley and Justin Kruger). So, less than 5 percent of all messages deliver the bare essentials of any accurate content. Combined with the probability that another 50 percent of these contain bad Netiquette or multiple mistakes or both, the final number of "bad" emails approaches 98 percent. If a sender places him or herself into this 2 to 4 percent tier of well-executed correspondences, his or her productivity, success, and even prestige will be effectively increased. As email continues to proliferate, the need to present well-executed messages will become even more essential.

The trend by many email/text senders has become one where, instead of looking to improve grammar, lucidity, or proper tone, the writer seeks ways to be "fashionably" incorrect. This process of chic incorrectness implies that the sender may know how to write a message properly, but, in fact, he or she is regressing into permanent habits with counterproductive results.

Example	**From:** The Dude [mailto:ssmith@anycompany.com] **Sent:** Monday, December 31, 2012 2:56 PM **To:** Gus Jones **Subject: Gus let's not meet ...** ...at your apartment but at Grand Central. Same bat time but an hour later. No need to call. Cheers, Sam Smith Anycompany Sr. Systems Engineer 555-303-7091 (c)
Explanation	In the above example, the author, Sam Smith, sent a message that has an alias. This may cause the recipient, Gus, to ignore the email. Secondly, by splitting the message between the subject field and the body, if Gus only sees this view he will not understand the nature of the email and may conclude that he should not meet. Thirdly, no confirming time is given, and whatever time the meeting has been scheduled for has been changed. So has the location. While being seemingly chic, the author has composed a very flawed email with a significant chance of being unproductive and possibly causing both parties to waste their time.

Good Netiquette

- Gives you an edge over others

- Empowers job-interview results and résumés

- Fosters traditional letter writing quality and effectiveness (see the Gettysburg Address then and now, at the end of this chapter)

- Offers a means to incorporate a sense of process to your communications

Netiquette last-stand resisters

There are those who resist--some arrogantly--Netiquette. It is beneath them, they have no time, it's inconvenient and uncool, they know best.

(Not so) personal letters

As briefly mentioned in this book's introduction, the aesthetic and emotional impact of personal letters is virtually eliminated by electronic mail. Additionally, many people compromise privacy by using work email to send and receive correspondence. Many users of their jobs' mail systems are unaware that most businesses have provisions for storage of all messages.

> **"The art of letters will come to an end before AD 2000. I shall survive as a curiosity."**
>
> - Ezra Pound

How would famous letters of the past look today? Here is one scenario:

Original text:	2013 version:
The Gettysburg Address	*The Gettysburg Address*
Four score and seven years ago our fathers brought forth on this continent, a new nation, conceived in Liberty, and dedicated to the proposition that all men are created equal.	TO: The US Congress FROM: POTUS CC: US Army RE: The battle of G'burg
Now we are engaged in a great civil war, testing whether that nation, or any nation so conceived and so dedicated, can long endure. We are met on a great battlefield of that war. We have come to dedicate a portion of that field, as a final resting place for those who here gave their lives that that nation might live. It is altogether fitting and proper that we should do this.	87 years ago the USA was born, so we all would B free. Now we're @ war. We just had a big battle & I wanted 2 pay tribute 2 the dead and wounded, of course.
But, in a larger sense, we cannot dedicate—we cannot consecrate—we cannot hallow—this ground. The brave men, living and dead, who struggled here, have consecrated it, far above our poor power to add or detract. The world will little note, nor long remember what we say here, but it can never forget what they did here. It is for us the living, rather, to be dedicated here to the unfinished work which they who fought here have thus far so nobly advanced. It is rather for us to be here dedicated to the great task remaining before us—that from these honored dead we take increased devotion to that cause for which they gave the last full measure of devotion—that we here highly resolve that these dead shall not have died in vain—that this nation, under God, shall have a new birth of freedom—and that government of the people, by the people, for the people, shall not perish from the earth. -Abraham Lincoln	The sacrifices speak 4 themselves and will B remembered. We need 2 make sure we finish the job ASAP. In this we'll B free. God bless the US. A. L.

Although the rewritten Gettysburg Address may seem overly simplified and a bit comical, emails of today produce results similar or even worse. This book is committed to assist all of its readers to take advantage of today's technologies by combining them with the positive attributes of traditional communication. By achieving this end, the reader will contribute to his or her own and others' successes.

Chapter I - Elements of an email

Netiquette language assumptions

In the pages of this book, obscene words and language, racist, derogatory, and even borderline terms will not be mentioned, as it is assumed these are never appropriate, and avoiding them is requisite to good Netiquette practice. It will be stated in different places in the book that, as tempting as it may be, adult or profane language should not be used. Some may believe that certain wording will facilitate getting a point or message across. However, such language is far more likely to produce negative results and will be a permanent record of a correspondence. There are always better ways to express a feeling, point of view, or response, even in the worst cases or with the rudest people.

Optimized email Netiquette involves a basic understanding of the core components of an email message, how they work, and their attributes. By simply learning these, anyone can improve their communication skills, reduce mistakes and mishaps, and produce emails that will enhance communication skills and benefit all email users, whether personal, general, or business. By consistently

"The smartest people can write the worst emails and those of less intellect can write the best."

- Paul Babicki

9

implementing simple, proper, basic email construction, any person of any age, social standing, demographic, or education can communicate better. As communication improves, a better world community results, with benefits all can experience and enjoy.

Have a need for speed? With the proliferation of email, texting, Twitter, and IM (Instant Messaging), the very basics of letter writing and English usage have dramatically suffered. Even the most learned of people have dramatically compromised their otherwise stellar or normal writing habits when using electronic communications.

The following is an example taken from the "Daily Mail," where considerable email shorthand is shown.

> 2 b, r nt 2 b dat is d Q wthr ts noblr nd mnd 2 sufr d slngs& arowz of outrAjs fortn r 2 tAk armz agnst a C f trblz, & by oposn nd em?

This example is, of course, text-speak for Shakespeare's Hamlet:

> To be, or not to be: that is the question. Whether 'tis nobler in the mind to suffer the slings and arrows of outrageous fortune, or to take arms against a sea of troubles, and by opposing end them?

The number of keystrokes that were reduced constitutes seventy in this example. At an average typist speed of 240 characters per minute, the time utilizing shortened words, omission of punctuation, basic format, capitalization, and basic grammar may marginally reduce input time, but actually can result in overall time loss. The average time saved in this example is less than twenty seconds. It would probably take the recipient longer to translate and read the shortened message. Many email readers may not recognize acronyms, Internet slang, emoticons, or abbreviations. Similarly, lack of punctuation may confuse text meaning, cause additional time to be spent rereading messages, or elicit a completely different meaning.

By contrast, a well-structured, Netiquette-compliant message will more likely deliver a lucid, easy-to-understand, effective message. This applies to personal and business messages alike. For individuals, accuracy with personal or basic communication will optimize relationships. For professionals or organizations, good Netiquette will convey professionalism, improve communication value, and reduce potentially damaging or embarrassing situations.

Ten precepts of Netiquette

1. No one ever gets fired for sending an email with the proper considerations.

2. Politeness works with even the rudest of people.

3. A policy and process of consistent correct email will contribute to actual time savings.

4. Use the three Zs—avoidance of **Z**ero tolerance, well-directed **Z**eal, and email **Z**en.

5. Personalize when appropriate.

6. Know when to apologize, and do so quickly.

7. Reply to every reasonable email promptly.

8. Avoid scolding, one-upmanship, and imperatives.

9. Include good news first.

10. Be proactive not reactive.

Chapter II - Basics

"Well begun is half done."
- Aristotle

Every email can be broken down into a recipient, a sender, a subject line, a body of text, a closing, and a signature. Even today, a large percentage of emails use plain text. Messages sent via phones are mainly plain text as well. Many senders will even go to the point of sending email in both formatted and plain text to accommodate recipients who might not have access to specific products (e.g., Microsoft Word, Outlook). Sending email in two formats is generally not recommended, as it will necessitate an attachment. Therefore, the best policy is to send only in a specific format, and, if unsure, use plain text. Obviously, one can respond to an email in the same format—or in plain text.

The From field

Most email automatically informs readers of the sender's name. Be mindful of how your name will appear when mail arrives in a mailbox. It will be the first item and impression your reader will have. Avoid all-lowercase names (e.g., john smith) and all-uppercase (e.g., JOHN SMITH) names, all initials (e.g., JQS), first-name only (e.g., Ed, Bill), nicknames (e.g., "The Crusher"), and titles (e.g., Admin).

The To address line

There are not a lot of variables that are inherent to address fields, but there are some subtle Netiquette rules that do apply. When addressing multiple recipients in the To field, use one of two formats to avoid potential affronts. When including two or more addresses, always position the person of rank first and the remainder of the addressees in the appropriate order. For example, if your To field includes the CEO, VP of human resources, and the manager of the mailroom, position these by rank to show both respect and to keep sensibilities in order. Address only those in the To field, not those in the Cc field.

If your To field has multiple addresses, or if the rank, company standing, or titles are unknown, simply list the addressees in alphabetical order by last name. If last names are not known, list addresses by the first character of their respective email address. At times, emails are sent with the addressor's name appearing in the To field. Although this procedure can have value, such as validating that the email service is operational, the name should be placed in the Cc field.

One of the core principles of Netiquette is to maintain the privacy of all. Many emails are sent to groups of people who may not have anything in common with anyone else in the group. Obviously, when sending to a block, some individuals will be upset that their names and email are exposed to the outside world. Not only is privacy compromised when their information is exposed, but the sender of the message has the appearance of being unprofessional, discourteous, or simply oblivious. Imagine when a To list includes dozens of individuals: sometimes these addresses will take up a page or more of an email. The above situation can easily be avoided by using the Bcc field. This excludes any recipient from viewing any other addressee.

The Cc field

All of the Netiquette outlined in the previous section applies to the Cc field. Care must be given for ensuring that protection of privacy is absolutely provided for in this field, which is visible to all recipients.

Those who are included here, as a rule, should be parties who have a direct interest in the subject. These people should not be addressed in the salutation or body of text, as their roles are passive, and are not expected to reply or take action unless explicitly asked to do so. If multiple responses are initiated, more addressees should not be added unless it is clear that the previous information is appropriate to those added. If this is not the case, the thread should be removed. Those who are included in the Cc field generally should not respond to the message without good reason.

Many add bosses, supervisors, or persons of higher rank in a Cc. Most of the time, this is for good reason. However, to include such persons to override an opinion, seek to impress, or have motives outside the issue at hand should be seriously considered because of the risk of changing the tone, range, or spirit of the communication.

Conversely, there are circumstances in email threads for dropping someone from a To, Cc, or Bcc field. Since threads can last for a number of messages, what began as a courtesy for some might become a nuisance to those receiving them. If there is diminishing or no further real significance for their involvement, Netiquette considerations should be given to determine if addressees should be dropped. Also, beginning a new mail thread might be the most useful way to disengage from longer threads.

Besides maintaining appropriate form, content, and consideration, good Netiquette goes beyond these disciplines. Do not Cc groups if the email is to a supervisor or persons of authority. This can be interpreted in a very negative way and can prove to be a significant embarrassment.

The Bcc field

Bcc refers to "blind carbon copy." It was originally used for paper correspondence. This option in sending emails is used to conceal the addressee from the complete list of recipients. The sender most often needs to ensure that multiple recipients of the message not see the names of other recipients. Usually, the Bcc recipient may see the email addresses of all recipients. Another use is for a very long list of recipients or a list of recipients who do not know each other, as used in large lists. Bcc is often used to prevent an accidental "Reply All" from being sent when a reply is intended for only the originator of the message.

Care should always be used in this function. No Bcc recipient should ever come into a thread. Similarly, the sender should be mindful of never addressing the Bcc addressee when naming other Cc recipients.

Adding Cc and Bcc recipients

It may be obvious to a sender who needs to be included in the Cc or Bcc fields. However, once a communication thread or a string of emails begins, there should be consideration and caution for adding to or deleting from the recipients. The most common Netiquette lapse is to hit a reply selection rather than a reply to all. The assumption should be made that the sender intended to have, at least, an initial response for all addressees. An obvious example of this would be a scheduling inquiry to a group. Clearly, if a reply is given to only one of a group, the results are likely to cause confusion or worse. If an omission to a reply is detected, the sender should resend the mail properly and excuse the omission.

Many recipients of an email will indiscriminately add or remove senders either to a Cc or a Bcc list. This behavior is not dissimilar to bringing an uninvited associate to an event. To act in this way necessitates either having the authority to do so or a reason that will be beneficial. Should the latter situation arise, proper Netiquette is to make sure new additions are approved and announced. Furthermore, if there are threats to remove, perhaps for security or redundancy purposes, this should be done so with proper considerations and permissions. A Bcc deserves careful consideration, particularly when interjected after a string of messages has begun. There may be reasons or circumstances when this is important, but to do this bears careful consideration and an explanation in a different email. Consider forwarding such a message as well. This allows for an explanation and is marginally more aboveboard.

Adding a superior to an ongoing thread

When a higher-level person of authority is added to a thread, the immediate tone will invariably change. Before adding a superior, careful considerations should be given since consequences might result in a change of tone. These dynamics may affect all or anyone in the thread. Simply put, there should be a compelling reason or reasons to add a higher person of authority, and any previous threads or attachments should be added or omitted based upon relevance. If the purpose of the manager or executive being added to a thread involves a dispute or complaint, it may be prudent to either go offline or limit the Cc list. In the case of a personal complaint or highly disputed situation, the additional person of authority may not welcome what he or she believes to be an inappropriate audience. One should also consider sending a separate communication to the person added explaining particulars. Otherwise, the person may be caught completely off guard or unaware of the preceding events. Clearly, this may result in an uncomfortable situation.

Being added as a Bcc

If one finds him - or herself as a Bcc recipient, it should be assumed the reason is necessary and appropriate. When this occurs, the utmost Netiquette should be exercised to ensure the discretion and confidence the sender has extended. Under no circumstances should a Bcc reply to a thread, in any form whatsoever.

Subject field

Besides the sender's name and company, this will be the first item a message reader will see. Therefore, this should never be blank. The action of not having a subject has only negative connotations. The least of these is that the author was lazy or neglectful. The worst of these is that the message is a possible spam (at least to the spam software). Either way, the initial reaction to any email omitting a subject will be negative. If it is indeed viewed this way, then the odds of the message being read by a first-time recipient surely decrease dramatically. If the message is important, such as a résumé, introduction, or emergency, the negative implications to the sender may be quite significant. So, always include a subject description. Provide proper punctuation, but do not include a period at the end.

Even when there is a subject description, it may not be adequate, appropriate, or accurate to the content of the message itself. Too short of a subject, such as "info," can also discourage someone from opening and reading the message. Conversely, a long email subject line might have a negative effect either for lack of interest (because of the way it is described), lack of clarity, or because it gives away too much of the content. As a rule, it is best to restrict the subject description from three to ten words. Ensure that a subject line is not the whole message with blank text in the email body. Some find it chic to split a message that begins in the subject line and continues into the text itself. This does not accomplish anything and, as often as not, it may be lost (or misunderstood) in the reader's transition from reading the subject line to opening the text itself.

In entering the subject-line content, it is best to accurately repeat content as well as present a bridge to something important to the recipient, such as "Schedule of your classes," or "Recap of our meeting today." Leave it to the body of text to explain attachments or provide expanded details. Make sure of the following:

A. Proper spelling and punctuation applies, as it does to the message body.

B. Do not use the message line as the total message.

C. When replying, be careful to keep the subject field relevant. Some messages can end up being Re:Re:Re:Re: (see sample below).

D. Be clear and concise, and keep content to a single line.

E. Be very careful of subjects that entice more than they deliver.

First email - no subject	**From:** Mark Crom [mailto:mcrom@NetiquetteIQ.com] **Sent:** Tuesday, July 31, 2012 2:56 PM **To:** Gecmen, Yagnesh x2348 **Subject:** Ok I figured out the ILMO....what ip can I use for your network. Mark Crom NetiquetteIQ, Inc. Sr. Systems Engineer 555-303-7917 (c)
Second email with one RE	**From:** Gecmen, Yagnesh x2348 [Yagnesh.Gecmen@TRS.com] **Sent:** Tuesday, July 31, 2012 3:04 PM **To:** Mark Crom **Subject:** RE: Use 149.83.200.27 **Yagnesh Gecmen** (201) 555-3488 TRS FINANCIAL SOLUTIONS
Third email with two RE	**From:** Mark Crom [mailto:mcrom@NetiquetteIQ.com] **Sent:** Tuesday, July 31, 2012 9:37 PM **To:** Gecmen, Yagnesh x2348 **Subject:** RE: RE: Hi Yagnesh, It was great working with you today. When you have a chance tomorrow can you send me a check report of the system - 250.88.200.26. Thanks, Mark

Fourth email with ...	**From:** Mark Crom **Sent:** Wednesday, August 01, 2012 10:24 AM **To:** Joe Berg **Cc:** Paul Babicki **Subject:** Fwd: RE: RE: RE: See below... Mark Crom NetiquetteIQ, Inc. Sr. Systems Engineer 555-303-7917 (c) Begin forwarded message: From: "Gecmen, Yagnesh x23488" <Yagnesh.Gecmen@TRS.com> Date: August 1, 2012 9:57:48 AM EDT To: Mark Crom <mcrom@NetiquetteIQ.com> Subject: RE: RE: RE: Hi Mark, I am looking to work from home tomorrow. Can you ask Joe to re-schedule the meeting? Thanks, **Yagnesh Gecmen** (201) 555-3488 TRS FINANCIAL SOLUTIONS
Fifth email of the string	**From:** Joe Berg [mailto:JBerg@NetiquetteIQ.com] **Sent:** Wednesday, August 01, 2012 10:26 AM **To:** Mark Crom **Cc:** Paul Babicki **Subject:** RE: RE: RE: RE: Mark, That's fine…before I attempt to reschedule, how does your calendar look for next Monday or next Thursday? Joe Berg Regional Sales Manager NETIQUETTEIQ, Inc. Phone: 555.234.1739

Grammar and punctuation in the subject field

The first word in the topic area should be capitalized. All other rules of grammar and punctuation should be followed as well, other than ending the topic with a period since many message descriptions are not complete sentences. Many presume that the rules of grammar, punctuation, and capitalization can be ignored. However, since this is the area that may present the addressee with his or her first impression of the sender, all of these items are even more critical.

We all want our messages to be read, and be read as soon as possible. There are many ways to accomplish this and just as many ways to fail in this. Terse and non-descriptive subject-line entries aren't likely to secure a recipient's interest and attention. Conversely, aggressive and pitch-like descriptions can easily produce their own negative effects. Be cautious of one- or two-word subject-line entries. Some of the most common are similar to "meeting," "request," "good morning," "position," and "something new." Specifically avoid informalities, unnecessary abbreviations, and emoticons (here especially).

When spell-checking, do not ignore the subject line. Many spelling errors occur here. If a person is responding to an email and finds an error, he or she should correct it; not to do so might result in anyone else reading the email thinking it is the responder's mistake. Clearly, one must be certain that any correction made is indeed correct. Be mindful of company names that mix capitalization unconventionally (e.g., iPhone, La-Z-Boy). When making corrections, do not chastise the sender's error. Remember that true Netiquette is not meant to force a process on someone's modus operandi. Netiquette works best by example, not criticism.

Signature address

In closing an email, every closing is a separate paragraph and should be ended with a comma.

1. Do not use programs that stamp every email.

2. Include as much useful information as possible.

3. Keep multiple signatures.

4. Avoid logos that are attachments, personal philosophies, politics, or religious themes.

5. Avoid signatures in a script, particularly if it is not one's own.

Options/flags

High priority means, "The sky is falling!" Some users present a high percentage of high-priority flags. If this feature is overused or not really viewed as important by one or more of the addressees, then future emails marked as such may be ignored altogether. Additionally, care must be given when addressing multiple parties in an email. What might be urgent to some may be of little relevance to others.

Rather than flagging, consider conveying a specific urgency, high priority, or desired attention by adding one of the following: "time sensitive," "please respond by mm/dd/time," "please read," or "your earliest attention is appreciated."

Email negatives

Email, for all of the qualities and benefits it delivers, has many aspects that counterbalance or supply more negatives as well as misconceptions of the supposed benefits. The inherent damage that poor email, lack of Netiquette, and simple bad habits can do is far greater than most people may realize. Just as many other innovations of technological progress over the centuries contributed beneficially to many, negative ramifications were also a less obvious result. These aspects will be expanded upon in the following pages.

Because communication between and among people and companies is becoming less reliant on face-to-face meetings, letters, or even telephone conversations, the emphasis has strongly shifted to email. For many, particularly younger people, this is now moving into texting and Twitter. A recent study from the Radicati Group estimates there will be an increase of email users from 3.9 billion accounts in 2013 with a volume of more than 500 billion messages per day, to 4.8 billion accounts by 2017. The profusion of messages necessitates greater pressure to reply and keep up with the volume.

These dynamics and circumstances are quickly transforming, within a single generation, behavior, trends, and standards that previously would have been several breaches of etiquette. Grammatical, spelling, and punctuation errors might easily diminish an author's credibility. Any student displaying the errors of composition and neglect of sensible structure endemic to many messages would fail even remedial English.

List of email negatives:

1. People lie and exaggerate more using email and feel more justified (Naquin et al., 2010).

2. Users believe they check and use email far less than they actually do.

3. Since online communication via email is not personal, inhibitions regarding some rules disappear or are negatively affected.

4. Many emotions, nuances, and dimensions of interpersonal communications are simply not available.

5. Bad habits and behavior patterns can take hold, particularly among younger users, and threaten to become inherent. These may be unwittingly manifested or perceived as strengths by the individuals.

6. Repercussions of bullying, postings, and blogs are increasing at alarming rates.

7. Fewer emails are replied to, and many of those replies are deficient (see chapter VII).

8. Fewer aspects of traditional communication occur.

9. Personalization is greatly diminished.

10. Respectful formalities can be omitted, and respectful tone is diminished.

Chapter III - Basic Content

"Make everything as simple as possible but not simpler."

- Albert Einstein

The purpose of an email is to communicate information of some kind, whether the content is positive or negative, casual or informal. Providing content in an effective manner is essential to ensure that the original intent is met.

Many items contribute to clarity and successful communication. Among these are appearance, grammar, vocabulary, structure, and choice of words. One spelling error can change the entire tone or perception of a message. Similarly, the visual presentation or order of facts can contribute to having a document marginally read or ignored.

Writing begins with fonts (typeface styles), spacing, paragraph structure, and essentially anything that makes up the view of an email. Fonts should be chosen with legibility being the key consideration. Type size should be appropriate to accommodate normal screens and not stylized so as to distract the recipients.

Common fonts

Ten- to twelve-point sizes are generally best to ensure optimal page fit and aesthetics. Changes from one style, size, or attribute should be kept to a minimum.

Font attributes

Every computer user is familiar with **bold**, *italic,* and <u>underscore</u>. To be effective, these should only be used to add emphasis or distinction. If overused, these attributes lose their effectiveness and can cause the reader to misunderstand the author's intent.

Text

Legibility is a key to email not only being considered to be read but also being read through to completion. Emails are not the vehicle for a creative or, worse, pseudo-creative page. There are three popular types of email formatting:

1. Plain text is still the most popular format for email, although less and less. As the name connotes, plain text provides virtually no formatting. Font color and bold typeface are not capabilities. Graphics page formats (such as columns), embedded programs, and multimedia are also not capabilities. In essence, plain text can be compared to a page composed on a typewriter.

2. HTML (hypertext mark-up language) is a page-description language where virtually any type of format or multimedia capability can be implemented. Full definitions and in-depth books, articles, and programming guides are plentiful and readily available. Many emails are written in this format.

3. "Enriched Text" FFC1341 or rich-text format (RTF) is from Microsoft and roughly provides MSWord-type capabilities to an email message. Microsoft owns and maintains the specifications. This format is widely used by MS Outlook users and provides interoperability among MS applications.

When selecting a format to send an email, the audience should be considered on an initial communication. If the email is outside of an organization, then plain text is the sensible selection. HTML format might be selected as marketing, promotional, or special-occasion communication. RTF should only be used when it is certain that the recipient uses Outlook. Some users compose a message in either RTF or HTML and add a plain-text-format attachment. This method is acceptable but may result in having a message rejected by anti-spam software or for other security concerns.

Types of email

Every email can be categorized into, arguably, eleven distinct types.

1. Personal
2. Introductory
3. Emotive
4. Informative
5. Commentary
6. Appreciative
7. Business
8. Spam
9. Invitation
10. Social
11. Formal

All of these share common Netiquette principles. Additionally, there are unique attributes and particulars that are specific to each category. As such, ensuring proper adherence and optimizing best practices within each email type ensures the best possible results. There are obvious differences, attributes, and nuances for each, and these will be discussed in this section.

1. Personal—Clearly, this type of email allows for the greatest flexibility, particularly with immediate family. Moreover, this type of email tolerates the greatest range of Netiquette interpretation. Despite allowing for exceptions, these should not go so far as to affect and carry

over into authoring other, more formal and structured compositions. Remember the rule of "composing emails consistently." The composer of personal emails should, at a minimum, keep within the basic rules of the ten parts of an email (see chapter I).

In a personal email, the salutation, body, closing, and signature can accommodate the most flexibility.

2. Introductory—This category of email can be a personal, business, or solicitation form. By its very name, the usual common thread is that it is a first-time message and might very well be one that is not expected by the recipient. Therefore, special attention must be given to the subject line and first paragraph in order to (a) be opened, (b) be read, and (c) be effective.

In terms of the subject field, an attention-producing or recognizable description is very important, particularly if the receiver has no reason to open the communication from seeing the user's name, organization, or Cc recipients. For example, if the message is by referral, the person should be mentioned in the subject line, such as the following:

"John Brown suggested I email you"

or

"Our mutual friend John Brown"

If there is not a common thread, a short and pertinent subject title is very important. The first paragraph of an introductory message should get straight to the issue. If there is a referral, the party should be mentioned right away:

"My name is Gus Jones. We have not previously met, and the reason for this email is that John Brown suggested I contact you."

Any amenities can be done later. Keep the overall email short and purposeful. State a next step or action, and specifically give the recipient a convenient way to reply.

3. Emotive—These types of email express some sort of emotion ranging from congratulatory to sympathy. These can be personal, business, or informative. They might be addressed to a single individual or to an entire company. Similar to the introductory email, these should be brief and provide an explanation or purpose of the email in the first sentence or paragraph. Any niceties or supplemental information can be added after this. Keeping the message focused is usually the most appropriate and most adherent to Netiquette. Requests for replies are usually not appropriate.

4. Informative—Emails of this ilk are sometimes personal but more often of a professional nature. Again, an informative subject line and direct statement of objective are critical to ensure a message is read. Replies should be encouraged and asked for. If the message is in response to a question having been previously asked, ask, "Does this answer your question?"

Many informative messages are solicitations for products, services, contributions, or other items. When these are legitimate in terms of requests, such as applications for newsletters, and will be of a repetitive nature, an option to unsubscribe is essential. When a message is a solicitation or response to one, the reason for the communication should necessarily be provided.

5. Commentary—These emails are among those that require the maximum Netiquette. Some of the primary reasons for this are that commentary emails might be political or otherwise have potential to spark heated debate.

A commentary message may also possess the quality of something similar to a review of a service or product. Certainly, all are entitled to their opinions, but this should be done within the rules of Netiquette. Remember, "emails are like diamonds; they last forever." Points of view can be expressed with proper language and decorum with equal or more comprehensive effect.

Example of disagreement:

Dear Mayor Hartman:

Your latest vote on spending is one I strongly disagree with. I will not be able to lend my support to it.

Respectfully,
Jim Williams,
Council Chairman

Example of agreement:

Dear Mayor Hartman:

Your latest vote on spending is commendable. I will lend you my full support.

Respectfully,
Joe Black
Councilman

6. Appreciative—Messages that offer appreciation are usually very welcome and some of the easiest to write. Nonetheless, there are emails of appreciation that are challenging and demand Netiquette compliance. Among these categories are subjects related to concession, personally unpopular decisions, or somewhat disappointing results. If a message of congratulation is given after a defeat, it should be one with facts and brevity. A negative tone or innuendo defeats the purpose and spirit of concessionary messages and forever might be remembered as sour grapes.

7. Business—None of the different email categories have more of a need to employ Netiquette than business-related emails. There are several areas within this book (see chapter X) where this topic is discussed. Basically, virtually all categories of Netiquette are important within the business email. The composition and distribution of business emails requires full attention and care. This is, in part, because no category of email, other than solicitation or junk mail, is typically as distanced interpersonally as this category is.

Any item related to a business email can have a profound or immediate effect in the business correspondence. This can be something such as the capitalization of a word, a punctuation mark, or the salutation.

Personal, casual, or even generic emails present far more tolerance to Netiquette mistakes. For example, an email sent to a relative in which his or her name is not capitalized will rarely be taken badly, but a similar error in a message sent to a stranger in a business context might easily be noticed and reacted to negatively. There is a great deal of detail involved with business. These will be presented in blog postings (see http://netiquetteiq.blogspot.com). The specifics will be characteristics of these forms:

A. Business to business

B. Business to customer

C. Marketing

D. Invitations

E. Business introductions

F. Cover—résumés

G. Cover—other attachments

H. Newsletters

I. Complaints

J. Employment—offer/acceptance/decline

K. Scheduling

L. Memorandum of understanding

M. Cover—proposal

N. Reference

O. Billing—reminders/invoices/other notifications

P. Promotion

Q. Letter of credit

R. Acknowledgment of receipt

S. Nondisclosure

T. Thank you

8. Spam—More than 85 percent of email is spam. Realistically, no user is fully able to avoid all the spam that he or she is sent, regardless of filters, removal requests, or other means of reducing these unwanted communications. Netiquette, in terms of spam, is primarily for the sender of messages. The lack of good Netiquette can actually result in a sender's email appearing to be spam. A lack of a subject field, unusual sender identifier, or improper subject-line content or email content can cause filters to relegate an important correspondence to a "junk" email box, return it, or drop the message altogether.

More on this topic will be addressed subsequently, but one very important item to conclude this section is that by having an email "bounced," the user may be blacklisted not only by a destination but also by a service provider or Internet security organization.

9. Invitation—Requests or invitations have rapidly proliferated from USPS mail to email. Netiquette is very important in sending or replying to invitations, just as "proper" traditional invitations and RSVPs were elaborately outlined and detailed by Emily Post and others. Most people enjoy having an engraved invitation, published on fine paper with very fancy typefaces, often in a cursive mode. Many of these include their own envelopes, helping the recipient comply with etiquette by replying rather than ignoring the invitation.

With the above considerations in mind, it is logical to assume that a well Netiquette-structured email invitation or evite will be appreciated, probably expected. Anything less than a message that is well constructed might serve a disappointment to the invitee. It is usually best to include one or even two attachments. The first would be a printed invitation, and the second would be a response form with the requisite particulars.

The focus of this section has been on those invitations that are more socially oriented. There are more types of invitations that will be blogged about and addressed in detail within other areas of this book. Among these types are meetings, educational sessions, and online presentations.

10. Social—These types of emails are growing in use with the proliferation of programs that focus on or have the capability of allowing all users to contribute and see threads and conversations. Marketers use email for bringing about dialogues among customers. A common use of this can be a user group for sharing experiences among fellow customers or consumers. Additionally, there can be requests for knowledge, referrals, or assistance. Another area where social email is used is with social bookmarking. This usually is a site with a compendium of links used to connect consumers or those seeking services to find those who have resources to fulfill these needs or requests. When connections are established, email exchanges can begin.

Social media and email—Social networking tools' utilization is rising astronomically. Because the issues of application capabilities, privacy, and availability can, at this point, not preclude transitioning away from traditional email, there is certainly a convergence of email, Twitter, YouTube, Facebook, and others. As more convergence happens, email will continue to have a significant part of these electronic communications.

11. Formal—These emails can share the attributes of other types, such as business, invitation, or social. All formal emails with correct Netiquette have the following characteristics:

A. Full identification

B. Strict, clear formatting

C. Concise descriptions

D. Minimum threads

E. No personalization

F. Spelling, tone, and grammar checked

G. Minimal acronyms

H. Factual information

I. Prompt follow-up

J. Avoidance of overuse of pronouns, particularly to begin sentences

The intent of formal emails is basically to be professional, sober, or strictly straightforward to minimize any possibility of error, perceived slight, or misinterpretation. Full objectivity is a critical component for realizing the best interest of the recipient.

Simple format rules

1. Try to limit emails to one page.

2. Keep paragraphs brief, but avoid having many short sentences.

3. Separate the closing.

4. Avoid multiple font changes, color changes, font size changes, and style changes, particularly in the middle of sentences.

In general, avoid parenthesis, characters, and unnecessary abbreviations such as thanx instead of thank you and msg instead of message; they save very little time. Contractions don't save much time (*don't* or *do not*, *can't* or *cannot*). Without contractions, your text improves considerably.

Basic content

Basic email text is not usually the vehicle for formal documents such as proposals, legal documents, and bills. These are conveyed as attachments by the vehicle of the email itself. When the exclusive purpose of the email is indeed the attachment, special care should be given to provide a description of what the document is, the purpose of it being delivered, and any other appropriate information. Additionally, any instructions, time-sensitive information, or content characteristics should be noted in the text of the email. Avoid using email for severance, bad news, or salary freezes. It is the best Netiquette.

Sentences

Email has significantly changed not only the ways we communicate, but it has changed some basic proclivities as well. The need, real or perceived, to compose or reply quickly to

"The better it sounds, the more it is trusted."

- Paul Babicki

email has reduced much of the structure that defined written communication in the past. Most senders will use at some point as little as one word or even an abbreviation (e.g., *FYI, OK*) as the entire content of an email.

In order to communicate clearly and effectively, some basic rules should apply to email sentences. Make sure that all sentences include the necessary parts of speech. All sentences should have at least a noun and a verb. Instead of "OK," say, "That is good," or "I will." Better still, use an adjective or adverb to better define a sentence. And even better, have a direct object for your sentences when appropriate. Notice the difference for answering a request to read a proposal:

OK

Definitely

I will

I will definitely read.

I will read it. (pronoun)

And best of all, use a noun object: "I will read the proposal." Using articles also enhances your communication. One of the most abandoned aspects of writing and grammar is the use of the article: "Please read attached" is written better when you say, "Please read the attached."

Unacceptable short emails

1. Sure.

2. You bet.

3. You're wrong.

4. No way.

5. Sorry.

6. Forget it.

7. Any stand-alone emoticon

8. Nope.

9. A single-word abbreviation (PLS, THX, and others).

10. Single acronyms (USPS, AARP, and so forth).

Conjunctions

By definition, these are words that connect or conjoin parts of a sentence. Most sources agree that the core conjunctions are the following: *and, or, nor, but, yet, for, since, because,* and *unless.* The key to proper use of conjunctions is to limit their use and to use them at the end of a string. The examples below show the incorrect and correct use of conjunctions in sentences:

Wrong:

The best email Netiquette consists of proper grammar, and tone, and good formatting of messages.

Right:

The best email Netiquette consists of proper grammar, tone, and good formatting of messages.

Chapter IV - Common Email Mistakes

> ## "I don't mind making jokes, but I don't want to look like one."
>
> - Marilyn Monroe

Placement is everything

Many emails provide information either within text, by providing a reference, attachment, or as a URL. Amazingly, many will place the main part of a message below the sender's signature. Although there may be logic behind it, this formatting may result in the critical theme being missed altogether. It is important to place this data where it can be seen on the initial display. It is also useful to offset the segment by indentation or to highlight it as colored text, italics, or some other standard method of distinguishing it.

Example: Wrong format for a link

From:	Sam Jones
To:	Gideon Baker
Cc:	support@netiquetteiq.com
Subject:	Our Support URL

Hello Gideon:

Your inquiry today is appreciated. Our blog URL is listed below. Please contact me if you have any questions.

Respectfully,

Sam Jones
Senior Engineer
NetiquetteIQ
Sales@netiquetteIQ.com
609-818-1802

HTTP://netiquetteiq.blogspot.com

Example: Correct format for a link

From:	Sam Jones
To:	Gideon Baker
Cc:	support@netiquetteiq.com
Subject:	Our Support URL

Hello Gideon:

Your inquiry today is appreciated. Our blog URL is listed below. Please contact me if you have any questions.

HTTP://netiquetteiq.blogspot.com

Respectfully,

Sam Jones
Senior Engineer
NetiquetteIQ
Sales@netiquetteIQ.com
609-818-1802

Many opinions exist concerning email mistakes. Some are quite obvious, others are subjective, and still others are subtle. One thing can unequivocally be stated: far too many mistakes are made. Some of these have been mentioned in other sections, and others require elaboration.

Example: Wrongly placed text to answer a question

From:	Sam Jones
To:	Gideon Baker
Cc:	support@netiquetteiq.com
Subject:	Answer to your question

Hello Gideon:

The NetiquetteIQ test measures a user's use of good Netiquette in creating or responding to email. Similar in concept, it looks at all of the components of email and scores based upon a defined set of standards.

What is your Netiquette IQ test?

Respectfully,

Sam Jones
Senior Engineer
NetiquetteIQ
Sales@netiquetteIQ.com
609-818-1802

Example: Correctly placed text to answer a question

From:	Sam Jones
To:	Gideon Baker
Cc:	support@netiquetteiq.com
Subject:	Answer to your question about our Netiquette IQ test

Hello Gideon:

Here is the answer to your question: *"What is your Netiquette IQ test?"*

The NetiquetteIQ test measures a user's use of good Netiquette in creating or responding to email. It looks at all of the components of email and scores based upon a defined set of standards.

Respectfully,

Sam Jones
Senior Engineer
NetiquetteIQ
Sales@netiquetteIQ.com
609-818-1802

It begins at home

Before electronic mail, letters were usually a one-to-one form of communication. Even with the introduction of copiers and other means of mail enhancement, any dissemination was still limited. Obviously, email has dramatically changed communication, thus making it possible and simple to send indiscriminate messages to multiple, hundreds, or even thousands of recipients. How many people suffer from far and faint acquaintances that produce both prolific and sometimes out-of-the-blue, detailed information on their lives, families, experiences, or beliefs? Many of these are embarrassing to the recipient and should be embarrassing to the sender as well.

When communications of this sort, which are personal, are conveyed unabashedly near and far, prejudices, political leanings, hugely subjective beliefs, religious, political, and detailed confidential information is provided to even those who do not have the slightest interest. Many friendly relationships can, as a consequence, be soured or ruined altogether. Contrast this with one-to-one correspondence where personalization, attention to detail, salient topics, and even confidential information might be delivered. Responses could be based on offering advice, sharing pertinent experiences, and even building, growing, and changing relationships.

Clearly, producing mass mailings to substitute for personal mail is a mistaken way to stay in contact in a healthy, growing, traditional way. In taking a few moments to address a recipient by name, inquiring about the person's health, children, or important family items, it gives a far more personal message and conveys a warmer sentiment.

Business mistakes

Email mistakes, abuses, and misuses cause hundreds of millions of dollars in losses every year. Although a significant portion of these events are not avoidable, a large segment is. In a sense, many of these problems lie strictly in the laps of corporations; namely, for a lack of process. Many employees honestly use the freedoms they are given de facto. These include access to personal accounts, no restrictions utilizing corporate email for personal use, and no written policy for dos and don'ts. Clearly, a well-defined, documented, and published corporate email policy (as well as Internet, Twitter, and texting) would address these.

Conversely, employees should be mindful not to purposely or otherwise abuse a service that they do not own and has not been set up for their convenience or benefit. If they do so, they are putting their jobs, reputations, and finances at unnecessary risk. Whatever they communicate via a company email account will likely be stored and accessible for many years.

One single inadvertent slip in a business email system can result in embarrassment to the corporation, other employees, or the individual sender. Participating in dissemination of recreational material such as jokes, images, multimedia, or other files may conceivably result in litigation or retribution. Purposeful or inadvertent transfer of confidential information, intellectual property, or competitive information can also result in damage to the corporation, management, or employees.

Part of Netiquette lies not only with the email composer but also with the owner of the infrastructure that provides the vehicle of the process itself. The incorporation of policy and procedure eliminates or reduces the risk of legal liability, violation of regulatory compliancy, and loss of reputation. Additionally, damage to confidentiality strains a company's IT resources and can adversely affect the business.

Chapter V - Spelling

"When our spelling is perfect, it's invisible. But when it's flawed, it projects strong negative associations."

- Marilyn vos Savant

Dictionaries and spell-checkers

Spelling checkers and dictionaries are the safety net of email and compulsory for Netiquette. Spell-checkers are built into many products, and there are many more that can be purchased and used separately. Building a personal, portable spell-checker is a very convenient, time-saving tool. Anyone who has replaced his or her computer or operating system has probably experienced a relearning and reloading process to incorporate words, acronyms, or even his or her own name into multiple spell-checkers. Since many do allow import/export, this function should be learned and maintained on a regular basis. Most of these products allow for exporting and importing other dictionaries. Additionally, there are products for specialty categories, such as medical, legal, and scientific applications. Most, if not all, dictionaries are heuristic and offer options for adding, deleting, and auto-correction. Many spell-checkers and dictionaries can be turned off, but there are few instances when this operational option should be disabled. Even though built-in spell-checkers are prevalent, using a freeware or packaged product is essential to everyone who wants his or her email read and responded to.

Dictionaries are also essential to proper Netiquette. Words used by senders may be misinterpreted and can distort the tone and meaning intended by the author. Any unclear definition should be looked up. Dictionaries are easy to find and use online. It is desirable to have a system-based dictionary for extensive offline work.

Thesaurus usage

Almost every person has used a thesaurus sometime during his or her time in school and afterward. It is an indispensable tool for any student, teacher, author, or other person who is involved in writing. Very few can say they have not been at a loss for the perfect word more than once!

Having and using a thesaurus is also an essential component of email Netiquette. It is always useful to find the best words to facilitate communication by bringing better clarity, succinctness, and variety of vocabulary to any email. Additionally, as has been stressed several times in these pages, giving thought to email correspondence invokes the best Netiquette, which in turn contributes to reducing the mistakes that poorly written emails can manifest.

One can acquire a thesaurus inexpensively in print or online or for no charge from many Internet resources. It is a resource worthy of constant use.

Misspellings

The most glaring mistake an email author can make is to misspell. Some mistakes may go unnoticed, while others may never be forgotten. A mistake may be laughable or embarrassing. One misspelled or misplaced word can change the tone of a correspondence. There is little, if any, excuse for misspelling any common word, since virtually all computer users have access to spelling checkers, dictionaries, reference sites, or even search engines. Even more importantly, correct spelling of proper names is tantamount in a business environment. Unlike a misspelling in an email address, such a miscue in the body of a message will certainly be noticed. Take care to look up and verify proper names, if there are any doubts. If significant spelling errors are missed and sent, it generally is a good idea to send a note back acknowledging the error.

Many email programs have dictionaries. Some will flag proper names. Some spelling checkers will also flag capitalization and acronyms with suggested alternatives. These or other spell-checkers might also contain online dictionaries that provide an option to add the word in question to it. Do not be concerned about too many dictionary entries. It is crucial to add names, not only to avoid a misspelling but also to save time. Many dictionaries will not include the spelling of people's common names. Moreover, last names are also not in dictionaries. To this end, it is good Netiquette practice to add important last names (first names also) to dictionaries. Include friends, acquaintances, business associates, or those to whom one will likely send emails.

Time—hourly

Time spelling has many variations. Many writers will spell time differently not only from email to email but also within an email itself! Generally, one should strive to be consistent. It is correct Netiquette to eliminate confusion, which can result in appointments being missed or other negative issues. With time spelling, often the simplest rendition is the correct one. The following rules have been cross-checked through various reference works and are given at the discretion of the author.

1. Using twenty-four-hour time representation should be avoided except in the military or scientific situations.

   Incorrect: 2315   Correct: 11:15 p.m.

2. Times for before or after midnight and noon should be spelled *a.m.* and *p.m.*, lowercase and with periods.

   Incorrect 1:08 A.M.   Correct 1:08 a.m.

3. When the exact hour of time is represented, do so without :00.

Incorrect: 2:00 p.m.   Correct 2 p.m.

4. *Noon* and *midnight* are adequate representations of time; the number is redundant, and *am* and *pm* are simply incorrect.

Incorrect: 12:00 noon or 12:00 midnight   Correct: noon, midnight

5. Using *o'clock* is rarely needed but is necessary when spelling a time, such as when beginning a sentence.

Incorrect: 6 p.m. is the kick-off time   Correct: Six o'clock is the kick-off time.

As evidenced above, most of the rules for denoting time are the simplest. Once again, if a consistent usage is maintained, the results will be beneficial.

Dates

Few who constantly misspell or misrepresent dates and times believe they are doing so, even though some will depict dates and times differently quite often—sometimes from one message to the next.

Just as with time, what can most commonly go wrong with misspelled (or incorrectly formatted) dates are missed appointments, payments, travel arrangements, and much more. Part of this problem also can be attributed to not providing full dates such as, "The game will be Monday, May 1" instead of "The game will be Monday." Why the emphasis here? If the sender actually has misrepresented the day of the week for whatever reason, the additional data might be a flag to the recipient to confirm the date. This works conversely as well: "The game will be on Monday, May 1," "The game will be on May 1," or even worse, "The game will be on the first of the month."

Do not use the ordinal form of dates. Correct: May 6. Incorrect: May 6th.

The following formats are acceptable for depicting dates. It should be noted that many countries differ from the United States for their respective date representations. Specifically, these instances can easily be found online.

Format	Example
MMMM D, YYYY Full month name, numeric day, comma, full year	October 16, 1951
D MMM YYYY Numeric day, short month name, full year	8 Jan 1955
MMM D, YYYY Short month name, numeric day, comma, full year	Dec 19, 1996
YYYY-MM-DD Four digit year, dash, two digits month, dash, two digits day	1999-02-22
D MMMM YYYY Numeric day, full month name, full year	17 July, 1918

Netiquette assumes that consistency is applied within bodies of email text. The following are a few more common suggestions.

1. Dates in quotes should not be changed.

2. When changing appointment times, both the originally and newly scheduled times need to be shown.

3. Approximate dates should be preceded by *c.* or *circa* and a year.

4. Ranges in dates, as in résumés, should include the earliest and last, separated by a spaced hyphen or en dash (–).

5. Decades should be represented by a simple plural, without apostrophes.

Incorrect: 1990's or 1990ies

Correct: 1990s

6. AD (or CE) and BC are capitalized, with no periods.

7. The date format used in the United States is MM/DD/YYYY. Most other major countries use date exceptions, including China, Korea, and Japan (using year, month, day). Other exceptions include Russia, most of Europe, and most of South America, which use day, month, year.

Numbers

Numbers are spelled and represented in many ways, not unlike depictions of time. Here are some basics that are accepted in the United States. Note that most numbers, dates, times, and forms of money vary outside the United States. What follows are some basic rules.

1. Beginning a sentence with a number should not normally be done. When it is necessary, spell out the number unless it is a year.

2. Spell out numbers one to ten, and use numerals for numbers above.

3. Use numerals for money. Make sure you include the cent (¢) and dollar ($) signs. Also use numerals for ages, percentages, page numbers, and decimals.

4. Hyphenate numbers from twenty-one to ninety-nine.

5. Spell out simple fractions such as one-half and three-fifths. Show mixed numbers as fractions like 14 ½.

6. Use either text or numbers for large round numbers.

   Correct: 7,000,000 or seven million

   Use numbers only for large figures of technical significance including sizes, measurements, clock time and coordinates. Correct: 7,245,666

7. It is necessary to use commas with numbers over 999.

8. For decimals with a value less than one, use a zero before the decimal point.

Correct: 0.17

For decimals with a value greater than one, a zero must follow a decimal point.

Incorrect: 6

Correct: 6.0

9. Use figures and words to distinguish adjacent numbers from each other.

Correct: 9 two-liter bottles

Telephone numbers use the following format: xxx-xxx-xxxx (parentheses not needed). Spell out the category: Home xxx-xxx-xxxx, Cellular xxx-xxx-xxxx. The number one or parentheses should not be used. This can cause problems if transposed. An extension should be represented in any of these ways:

> 555-555-5555 x-123
>
> 555-555-5555 ext-123
>
> 555-555-5555 extension-123

International telephone codes

Almost every country has a different way of representing telephone numbers. If a representation for an overseas number is given, it should be written in full format, including "011," so that there is not a need to look up the country code when dialing overseas from the United States. In short, proper Netiquette provides as much information as possible for the native reader to most easily place a call.

Letters as phone numbers

Many companies represent phone numbers as letters. Although this may allow for an easy (or easier) way to remember a telephone listing, it invariably increases the time required to place a call. The proper way to have a listing with letters is to also show the corresponding numbers-only depiction:

1-NETIQUETTE

1-638-478-3883

Acronyms

Since most email senders use capitalization for acronyms, there are a few items to keep in mind. The first is to be consistent. Many spell-checkers will not flag all-capital words, with the assumptions that these are acronyms and therefore correct. If one misspells an acronym, the checker may not intercept it. Additionally, one should be careful not to add a word that might either be one of the words of the acronym (e.g., *HIV virus*) or a synonym for one of the words (e.g., *CD disk*). Finally, words that are included in any acronym that is short should be capitalized (e.g., *DOD* not *DoD*).

Chapter VI - Punctuation

> "The writer who neglects punctuation, or mispunctuates, is liable to be misunderstood for the want of merely a comma, it often occurs that an axiom appears a paradox, or that a sarcasm is converted into a sermonoid."
>
> - Edgar Allan Poe

The following chapter on punctuation is not intended as a reference work. Simply, it is a brief overview to remind and encourage users to be aware of the basic uses of punctuation, as they are a vital part of Netiquette.

One of the most overlooked aspects of email is punctuation. If used thoughtfully and properly, punctuation will add readability to one's correspondence. If underused or not used at all, its misuse can contribute to misunderstanding data, content, or intention. Additionally, proper punctuation adds both a professional appearance and sense of personalization and concern for the recipient.

Periods

Always have a period (or sentence-ending punctuation mark) at the end of a sentence in the body of an email. Periods are not necessary in message description fields unless there are two sentences. Be careful not to have a misplaced period. This may cause some spelling and grammar checks to insert a capital letter for the succeeding word. The period may only be a dot, but what a powerful dot! It is used to separate sentences. Reading a passage not delimited with periods would be extremely tiresome, and the meaning would become quite ambiguous. So, one must remember, whether the sentence is short or long, it *must* conclude with a period (or other sentence-ending punctuation mark). Periods have also been used traditionally to indicate an abbreviation: for example, *a.m.* and *p.m.* In modern usage, however, this is becoming more infrequent, and abbreviations now regularly appear without periods: for example, *am* and *pm*.

Commas

These marks represent the most errors in virtually any written communications. They can be underused, overused, or even both. The use of commas should be kept to a minimum in emails. The appearance of too many may mean there are sentences that are too long, more modifiers than are needed, or a combination of both. If one follows a simple set of rules for use of commas consistently, the quality of emails will be improved. Mastering the versatile comma can transform one's writing. Here is a brief list of some of its most important functions:

Itemizing	On the stationery order, pencils, erasers, pens, staples, paper clips, and notepads were listed.
To set apart persons and names	John, my friend, what are you doing here?
Adding an additional thought	The wedding was, on the whole, very enjoyable.
To set off comparisons	The louder she spoke, the more he shouted.

Repeat punctuation

Ellipses, which are a connected series of three periods or dots (…), are fine when used properly, and they can enhance the tone or composition of a communication. For other punctuation marks, repetition should not be used. The most common abuse of this is with exclamation points (!!!) and question marks (???). These should be avoided because even with the most sincere intentions, using these can connote a sense of anger, condescension, impatience, or sarcasm. Multiple uses of exclamation points or question marks are rarely applied in business communication or literature. The three-dot ellipsis is primarily used to indicate missing words or phrases. It can be subtly used in these instances to indicate an unfinished thought.

An implied word or phrase the reader is expected to know	He was about to jump, but then he thought...
Words or phrases omitted from a quotation	When asked why he was afraid of flying he said, "What goes up, must..."
Disjointed speech	He was so shocked, he could only mumble, "What the... I mean to say... Where in the..."

Apostrophe

Apostrophes are used in two different ways.

1. to indicate possession

2. to indicate missing letters when words are shortened (contraction) Example: "Let's all go in John's car."

The apostrophe in the word *Let's* indicates a shortening of *Let us*, and the apostrophe in *John's* indicates the car belongs to John. The position of the possessive apostrophe can indicate singular or plural:

"Stand outside the girl's school." (One girl)

"Stand outside the girls' school." (A group of girls)

So to use apostrophes without grammatical catastrophes, think which use is correct. Is the apostrophe needed to show possession or to show contraction? If neither, then an apostrophe is not needed.

Asterisk

The asterisk is a reference mark indicating that a footnote or explanatory paragraph appears somewhere else on that page, generally at the foot of the page. See this example.*

---

* Another use of the asterisk has developed: to indicate swear words without being objectionable yet conveying the same force meant by the speaker; for example, "He replied, 'Don't be such a b**** fool!'"

Bracket

The functions of the square bracket and the round bracket (parenthesis) are quite different. Square brackets have limited use, primarily being used in publishing to indicate a comment or clarification from an editor or other authority; for example, "The press secretary said, 'He [President Obama] was about to embark on a tour of the Far East.'"

Bullets

Bulleted lists are extremely effective in capturing the interest of your audience. Persons who browse the Internet want to find information quickly. They want to be able to read easily without having to wade through pages of text. Bullets (e.g., •) direct the eye to the main points quickly. They encourage writers to be brief, stating the main point in a few words or a phrase. They summarize a list of points or conclusions.

Capitals

The main rules for using capitals are as follows: Capitalize proper nouns; for example, "Take a trip to New York City." Capitalize the first word in a sentence. Capitalize the first letter of each word in a title except for articles, conjunctions, and prepositions. Capitalize a person's title when it comes before their name; for example, "Doctor Jones." Capitalize the first word in a quoted sentence; for example, "Derek said,

'That book is worth reading.'" Caution: Do not capitalize everything in a heading. While the desire may be to attract attention, the effect can be tiresome and overdone. One other very basic rule of Netiquette is to never use all capital letters in a word or sentence, e.g., JOE, LISTEN TO ME, or WRONG. The use of capitals implies anger on the sender's part. There are easily many other ways to politely show urgency or attention. Remember, some spam filters may block words or sentences which contain all capitals since these may also appear as promotions, such as FREE.

Colon

The colon is generally used to introduce something that follows. Here are some places where a colon is well used, such as to introduce a list. For example, "Send the letter to the following departments: Sales, Marketing, and Admin." A colon also can introduce a quotation, question, or conclusion; for example, "The conclusion of the matter was reached: Let bygones be bygones." Please note that the statement immediately preceding the colon should be a complete sentence.

Dash

The dash can be more powerful than a comma or a semicolon or parenthesis. However, it should be used judiciously. Overdone, it can make a passage seem disjointed. What is the difference between a dash and a hyphen? The longer dash (—) is used in the construction of sentences. A hyphen (-) is used in the construction of words.

The dash can be used to in the following ways.

Example	The room was decorated with three strong colors—blue, green, and red.
Pause	The train arrived as expected—one hour late.
Interrupt	"I must ask you, sir, to—well, I'm sorry—to leave!"

| Extend a sentence | The heckler hurled abuse at the speaker—then quietly sat down. |
| Separate a list | She collected all her tools—brushes, oils, palette, cloths, crayons, and canvass—and started to paint. |

Exclamation

Judicious use of the exclamation mark adds emphasis to important statements. Overuse kills its effectiveness. So think twice before using an exclamation mark. Here are some situations where nothing but an exclamation mark will give the same sense:

To command	Get back!
To convey irony or reverse meaning	You must be joking!
To emphasize true excitement	You are great!
To convey strong emotion	That was terrible!

Hyphen

Hyphens are used to join two associated words. To illustrate, the hyphen in "man-eating tiger" changes the meaning entirely from "man eating tiger." In the first instance, we are talking about a tiger that has a taste for humans. In the second, we are talking about a man who has a taste for tigers. Hyphens are also used as guides to pronunciation (*anti-intellectual*); to divide a word at the end of a line (which is not relevant for emails); for emphasis (*I said, "I'm f-r-e-e-z-i-n-g"*); and to separate grouped names (*Anglo-French Alliance*).

Parentheses

Parentheses (round brackets) insert relevant, additional, but non-essential material into a sentence, and the sentence would still read smoothly without it. Here are some uses for parentheses:

To add information	The house was in an ideal location near the sea (just a five-minute walk), so there was no problem in getting tenants.
To add afterthoughts	The speaker was totally unprepared for this kind of audience (or so it seemed).
For clarification	Their action was in violation of the Terms and Conditions (page 2, paragraph 3) they had signed.
To add personal remarks	They were so proud of their newly decorated apartment (to me it seemed a little tacky), they insisted on giving every visitor a guided tour.
To show options	Please put the document(s) in the tray on the secretary's desk.

Question mark

The most obvious use of the question mark is at the end of a sentence that asks a direct question: "Where are you going this weekend?" However, when an indirect question is raised, a question mark is not needed: "She asked me if I enjoyed her cooking." The question mark can also be used to create other effects, such as to invite an answer: "This seems the wrong color, don't you think?"

Quotation mark

Quotation marks are used to indicate direct speech. They are extremely important in conveying accurate meaning. Without them, it can be hard to know who is speaking or who is being spoken about, or whether the quotation is a paraphrase or direct speech: "Tom said, 'It was his fault we were late.' "Tom said it was his fault 'we were late.'" In the first example, Tom is blaming someone else. In the second example, he is taking responsibility himself. The quotation marks make all the difference to the meaning. Should ending punctuation be within the quotes or outside the quotes? In American English, all punctuation marks except for colons and semicolons come before closing quotation marks at the end of a sentence. Here are a number of instances where quotation marks are effective:

To indicate a title for a short work such as a song, story, or episode.	He started reciting Shakespeare's "My Mistresses' eyes are nothing like the sun."
To indicate doubt or disbelief	The clinic had one "doctor" on duty that evening.
To indicate that a word or phrase should not be taken literally	New synthetic fibers have made "grass" playing surfaces very durable.

Semicolon

The uses of semicolons are numerous. Here are the main ones:

To join words, phrases, or sentences, and to separate word groups that already contain commas	The committee was made up of M. Baker, president; J. Smith, vice president; B. Jones, secretary; and W. White, chairman.
To join two complete, independent clauses or sentences	He just scraped past the finishing line by a hair's breadth; nevertheless, he won!
To emphasize opposite statements and contrast	The house looked beautiful after the renovation; pity, about the garden.

A good way to remember when to use the semicolon is that syntax, not content, determines semicolon use.

Forward slash

The forward slash (/) is sometimes referred to as a solidus or virgule. It has limited functions. It's used primarily to indicate options—such as "That will be his/her choice," and to abbreviate: for example, "care of" can be depicted "c/o." The forward slash is also used as part of a network address or URL (e.g., *http://www.netiquetteiq.com*). The forward slash can be used several times in a single sentence: "who/what/when/where." In such instances, commas might be used instead.

Back slash

This punctuation (\\), sometimes referred to as a reverse solidus, is used primarily in computer programming and scripts and rarely in standard English.

Chapter VII - Ambiguity

"The question is, said Alice, whether you can make words mean so many things."

- Lewis Carroll

ecause of email, billions of email senders are connecting and communicating with far more numbers of people than was ever deemed possible a short time ago. In a few seconds, anyone can send more emails than a person could send regular letters in a lifetime. As mentioned in the introduction of this book, email is by far the least effective form of communicating between and among people. In a recent article, "Can We Resolve Ambiguity by Email?" Daniel Verhoeven wrote,

> *Email cannot replace the fullness of face-to-face communication; it is only an extra channel with limited utility. It's useful in situations we can express ourselves unequivocal, but it cannot resolve ambiguity. In such a situation email rather adds to chaos.*

In light of this dynamic, Netiquette is critical to help minimize email ambiguity. By maintaining lucidity, clarity, and consistency, which constitute the core of Netiquette, ambiguity can be minimized, eliminated, or reduced when it does occur. Just as with other processes, Netiquette will produce positive results when used. If it is ignored, all or in part, more negative results (i.e., increased ambiguity) are likely to occur.

When people do not know each other, ambiguities arise more often. Email contributes to ambiguity by

- reducing communication to only a few paragraphs

- increasing Internet language overhead, which includes abbreviations and shortcuts

- multitasking during message composition, which contributes to carelessness and mistakes

- assumptions that errors are acceptable concluding that something said verbally can be equally understood in email

Most common words to avoid ambiguity

The words only, even, exactly, hardly, and just are limiting modifiers. They must be placed immediately before the word they describe; if they are not, more confusion can result.

> **"Non-ambiguity is the shaping force of reality."**
>
> - Joseph Pierce

Ten quick steps to reduce ambiguity

1. Whenever possible, limit all email requests, tasks, or questions to one item.

2. After answering questions or fulfilling requests, ask if the responses or actions have satisfied the recipient. It should be stated that any outstanding question or item left unclear will be elaborated upon as needed, and the recipient should be welcomed to request better information.

3. Avoid multiparty threads with multiple-choice options or responsibilities.

4. If an email is unclear or ambiguous, the recipient should immediately ask politely for clarification. This is far better to do than providing an answer to what is perceived as one thing but actually is intended as another. If an explanation does not provide clarification, it is still good Netiquette to ask again.

5. Make certain punctuation is used correctly. Parentheses are very helpful in framing clarification.

6. One should be prudent with and use pronouns correctly.

7. Trailing or leading modifiers are best used very carefully (see chapter V).

8. Watch for dangling participles. One example of this that will always be remembered is: "Please don't leave me dangling." Another example with a sentence is: "With limbs dangling, the crowd cheers the vulnerable boxer."

9. Terse answers to questions can be especially prone to ambiguity.

10. Should one deem that a sent email may have ambiguity potential then a proactive correspondence should be sent asking the recipient to verify that the message is clear.

Misused or misplaced identifiers

It would be possible to have an entire book dedicated to the different categories of grammatical ambiguities. Many people are not able to define these. Moreover, many would be hard-pressed even to specifically identify them. But most would feel awkwardness or need to reread sentences where these mistakes occur.

The category of "identifiers" will be briefly addressed here to assist email composers in minimizing ambiguity and increasing clarity. There are four specific types of these, which will be addressed in this section.

1. Misplaced leading modifiers

2. Misplaced trailing modifiers

3. Serial modifiers

4. Dangling participles

For the purpose of brevity, a brief definition and correct/incorrect examples follow:

1. A **leading modifier** is any word or words that come before the word they modify, usually directly before.
   Correct: Wearing the red uniform, the player was visible from far away.
   Incorrect: Wearing the red uniform, I was able to view the player from far away.

2. **Serial modifier**—This term defines a word or group of words describing more than one person, place, or thing.
   Correct: All males/females less than twelve years old must be accompanied by their parent.
   Incorrect: All males and females less than twelve years old must be accompanied by their parents.

3. **Trailing modifier**—This is the opposite of a leading modifier in regard to its placement in a sentence.
   Correct: The one I saw score the goal was the player wearing the red uniform.
   Incorrect: Wearing the red uniform I saw the player score a goal.

4. **Dangling participle**—This term probably is the most used and least understood of all. Essentially, dangling participles are modifiers that do not have a subject in the sentence. They do not relate to the noun they should be modifying, as evidenced below.
   Correct: Arriving at the game, I saw my favorite player wearing the red uniform.
   Incorrect: Arriving at the game, wearing a red uniform was my favorite player.

Whoever can gauge and set a consistently appropriate tone in electronic communication will have a tremendous influence on the outcome. The greater this attention and practice are, the more successful the communications and the better the atmosphere will be.

Chapter VIII - Email Policy

"In modern business it is not the crook who is to be feared most, it is the honest man who doesn't know what he is doing."

- William Wordsworth

Epolicy and Netiquette are closely interrelated. Most epolicies, whether they are personal, those of small groups or large corporations, have core Netiquette principals. A policy is as defined by the Merriam-Webster dictionary: "a definite course or method of action selected from alternatives and in light of given condition to guide and determine present and future decisions." Although the term *epolicy* has not been officially designated as a real word by certain reference works, it is a term generally used by many to reflect the procedures for maintaining email, messaging, or Internet usage rules.

Essentially, epolicies are put into practice in order to provide rules, guidelines, security, adherence to laws, optimization of resources, and standards by anyone using email. As the proliferation of email grows, so does the necessity of epolicies. Many businesses have a complete set of standard epolicies in place. The following sections identify and define the key epolicy areas.

Epolicy security

Security is a key core element of an effective corporate epolicy. Failure of effective security with email can result in fraud, public embarrassment, compromised files, loss of business, or termination of employment. Email security and policy can encompass entire books on their own. Still, certain basic requisites and processes should be stated and instituted with qualified, professional security-engineering resources employed to institute the proper products' implementations and to manage these processes. Having the following reporting are some of the essentials of good email security: firewalls, scanners for viruses, written Netiquette policy, and employee education. Egroups and companies should verify forensic tools are in place and available to provide for troubleshooting and root-cause analysis of problems and performance.

Password access and protection

All corporate email accounts should have password access and the means of changing these on a regular basis. An effective system of monitoring and logging usage and traffic also should be an essential part of email and epolicy operation. Passwords should be "strong," meaning that they are uncommon alphanumeric combinations together with upper- and lowercase characters as well. When attachments of confidential information are sent, these files should also be password protected, with the password conveyed separately to the files' intended reader. In cases where email is accessed from computers not assigned to employees, browser caches, history, and passwords should be deleted. (See appendix L for the most common weak passwords.)

Testing

Good email security policies should include a test system that can be used on a regular basis. Many products and services are available to provide full email policy security testing. Some of the specific features that should be considered for testing and protection include the following:

- Spam software—Some type of spam testing should be implemented. These tests will usually trigger a spam filter.

- EXE attachment files—These are executable files, which can be a source of malicious program attacks.

   Zip files—Attachment compressed file utility, which can contain compromising files or programs.

Privacy

Because large corporations cannot rely on individual adherence to policies, certain measures, including monitoring of email, are necessary. Legal rulings long ago determined that employees do not have expectation of privacy in regard to email. All employees should be informed of this. Employers should be educated as to the potential damages, both personal and corporate, of abuses of Netiquette and email policies. It is appropriate to require employees to sign off on their knowledge of corporate epolicies, not only with privacy but also with all of the components associated with incoming and outgoing messages. Legal issues of email are discussed in greater detail in chapter XII. There are several federal laws that allow and govern employer email monitoring. The most-used is the Electronic Communications Privacy Act (ECPA).

Creating a personal email policy

All email users should incorporate a personal epolicy as de facto to effectively and safely communicate via email. The following are specific examples that are focused upon personal email protection, although many organizations incorporate these policies. The needs and consideration of these entities require substantial components that are far more detailed. These should be addressed separately.

Necessary or strongly recommended items	Optimal items
Netiquette adherence	Grammar-check software

Firewall	Personal dictionary
Automated archiving	Tone-check
Spell-check	Spam filters
Virus scanner	Email security
Personal signature template	Disclaimer
Schedules and processes for • replies • archiving • clearing all mail files • password protection	Thesaurus
Auto replies	Calendar for mailing reminders
Family access and usage	Templates
Email content scanning both incoming and outgoing email	Rules for checking email in public, at meetings, on personal time, and during specific hours of the day
Updating software patches	Rules for children's and family usage similar to those above

Email policy objectives

1. **Business objectives**—These are the providing of rules and procedures to conduct professional transactions and beneficial relationships both intra- and extra-company. Netiquette is an integral part of these.

2. **Ethical behavior guidelines**—These are the core principles that are the basics of fair and honest behavior alongside established email and Internet policies, including proper Netiquette. These should be, in part, voiced in the company mission statement. The importance of ethics in the workplace and marketplace are critical to every company and employee.

3. **Legal guidelines**—Every company should have access to appropriate legal counsel. Every company should have full familiarity with the legal issues of email. Moreover, these should be documented and reviewed on a consistent basis and put into writing with approval of qualified legal counsel. Proper subsets of these should be provided to all employers, contractors, and business partners. Maintaining a company policy guidebook with Netiquette and email codes of conduct and ethics is desirable as well.

4. **Productivity management of email**—Many studies suggest that company resources are given to unnecessary and often detrimental email usage. The implementation of workplace policies that define company-based rules of email are not only beneficial to companies to reduce bottom-line costs but are conducive to good work habits by individual employees as well. The following are the various items to implement, in some optional measure, to increase workplace productivity:

   - Netiquette

   - Response time frames for customer, company, and miscellaneous emails

   - Personal usage limitations

   - The limitation of the use of private email accounts

   - Sufficient hours to access/reply/compose emails

   - Educate users with products such as NetiquetteIQ. See www.netiquetteiq.com.

Processes

Any defined policy will function far better with a well-planned and defined corporate process. Rules, procedures, and usages without a cohesive and appropriate process will not only operate less effectively but also may end up being counterproductive. The following are core elements to consider when putting a formal epolicy in place:

1. Planning

2. Testing

3. Educating

4. Implementing

5. Monitoring

6. Managing

7. Reporting

8. Optimizing

9. Reviewing

10. Revising

Plan—Outline a set of internal and external epolicy items and actions. These may be multiple policy engines for different groups, departments, or company areas.

Test—Find suitable methods of testing and validating the policies set forth.

Educate—Provide guides and written statements to employees clearly defining the rules and process of the company's epolicy and Netiquette.

Implement—Install the epolicy, and verify that the appropriate personnel are notified.

Monitor—Measure the effects of the epolicy. This can be accomplished using any number of software products.

Manage—An assigned group or groups should be given the responsibility to manage how email is secured, delivered, and properly stored.

Report—Provide reporting of key information. This should be done on a regular basis.

Optimize—Ascertain those areas that can be improved upon. Incorporate best practices for mandated laws and regulations.

Review—Schedule reviews at regular intervals.

Revise—If specific parts of the process are deemed necessary to change or if new parts are needed, cycle through the appropriate process again.

Epolicy dos and don'ts for corporations

Do	Don't
Make Netiquette the foundation of your epolicy	Allow too much time to elapse between policy reviews
Implement strong email security	Compromise enforcement and allow formats not company approved
Scan all email for viruses	Maintain public files with personal information
Scan all email for content	Purge emails quickly. Archive for several years or as legally required
Store and archive all email	Share customer information
Know and adhere to all laws	Assume offline laws apply to online laws
Educate employees	
Be clear in all aspects and provide epolicy rules in writing	
Have employees sign off on acknowledging epolicy knowledge and understanding	
Have password access	
Have SSL (Secure Socket Layer) in place	
Post privacy email policy where deemed appropriate	

Chapter IX - Replies and Forwarding

"Prepare your proof before you argue."

- Jewish Proverb

Replies and forwarding

Replying to emails requires the same level of attention, consistency, and proper Netiquette as a newly composed message. Additionally, replies to emails can sometimes be in haste, far too long or brief, mistakenly assumptive, or disingenuous. The following sections refer to the basic areas to give attention to proper Netiquette replies. One should not ever assume that the recipient will fully understand a reply without at least a short recap, explanation, or reference.

Times to reply

Allow time for others to reply who are in higher positions, are more involved, or in some other way take precedence. Reply times are subjective, based upon many factors. Nevertheless, it will almost always be better to reply a bit too soon than a little too late. Negative or bad news is almost always best done promptly but also with respect to timing such as holidays, special events, or times that may be difficult.

Replying

1. Always include the original, but avoid threads.

2. Do not reply to spam.

3. Do not forward jokes.

4. Answer swiftly.

5. Answer all questions in order.

6. Avoid messages with large attachments.

7. Compress attachments of significant size.

8. Keep your signature above the reply quotation.

9. Before replying angrily, think of the worst, most regrettable or most embarrassing email you have ever sent.

10. Replies should not be sent with attachments from previous messages, particularly threads, without proper reasons.

11. Avoid sending two or more separate emails to reply to a single correspondence unless one is correcting, replacing, or adding important information. Such second messages should state why another message is being sent, preferably in the subject line. One example would be as follows:

Subject: *Please disregard the last message.*

Subject: *Correction for our recent email.*

Simple reply

Replies should be in complete sentences and, when answering a question, should be a clear continuation. This is particularly necessary when a reply is later than half a day.

General email reply rules

1. "Down-editing"—replying point-by-point within text

2. "Top-posting" replying—replies should be at the top of the email, and superfluous information is best removed.

3. Numbering of multiple replies—a clear delineation should be made.

4. It is good Netiquette to reply in the proper order and context.

5. As stated previously in this book, avoid replying with single words or incomplete sentences. If one is replying to questions, all should be answered by an acknowledgment, even when the replier does not know the answer.

Reply to multiple people or a group

Take care when a reply requires two distinct answers. The best way to approach addressing multiple recipients is to define the content of the email. An example would be as follows:

Dear John and Joe,
Thank you for the information. I will address both of your re-spective concerns in two separate paragraphs that follow…

The following is a matrix listing general time frames for replying to emails in keeping with good Netiquette.

	Professional	Casual	Personal	Miscellaneous
Time to reply	1–24 hours	1–3 days	Anytime within reason	1–3 days
When unsolicited	As necessary	As necessary	As necessary	As necessary
When marked urgent	As quickly as possible or within requested time	As quickly as possible or within requested time	As quickly as possible or within requested time	As quickly as possible or within requested time
Employment or money matters	As quickly as possible	N/A	As quickly as possible	As quickly as possible

Auto-reply	Immediate	1–2 days	Any reasonable time	Any reasonable time
Invitation	1–24 hours	1–24 hours	1–24 hours	1–24 hours

The time between an email delivery and response can be a critical factor in how your message is received and perceived. There are several items to consider regarding response time.

1. *Severity shown by the sender*—If a time-sensitive aspect has been given to a communication, clearly consideration should be given to respond quickly.

2. *Standards and goals for the amount of time to take to respond*—Obviously, times will differ depending upon a message being business, personal, or casual.

3. *When thanking someone*—One thank-you is sufficient. One "You're welcome" is optional.

4. *When not to reply*—As a rule, try to reply to all legitimate emails in a consistent time line. While one should always reply when specifically asked to, one sometimes should not reply on demand, such as when not physically possible (no email access) or after an exchange of *thank you* and *you're welcome* messages has transpired. Remember, it is not always necessary to have the last word.

5. *More Information*—Auto replies

   When planning to be away from email for a significant period of time, usually a full business day or longer, setting an auto-reply message for business accounts is highly recommended. The following items should be included:

   A. A brief statement, such as "I am currently out of the office…"

   B. The date of your return

   C. Whether you will have any email access

D. Options for your senders to take (e.g., contacting an individual or group who will be most likely to provide assistance)

6. *Threads*—A "thread" is a sequence of responses to an initial email or message posting. When responding to an email, it is almost always necessary to include at least the last part of a thread. Beyond that, long threads can prove cumbersome or lose their original thought or meaning via "threadjacking." Threadjacking is a term referring to a situation where the original message content or theme is significantly or completely changed.

7. *Another common error is "message switching,"* where an older message is used to reply to a newer one, often without the subject-matter title being changed! To employ this method may save a few seconds, but it certainly does not convey any positive impression. Moreover, it will imply to some a laziness or sense of disorganization toward the composer. If you must use an older message with a different subject and content, simply change the subject-matter reference, and delete the unnecessary content.

First email	**From:** Paul Babicki [mailto:paul@TabulaRosa.net] **Sent:** Tuesday, October 16, 2012 2:16 PM **To:** Serkan Gecmen **Subject:** NetiquetteIQ Score Hello Serkan: Please send me my NetiquetteIQ rating. Thank you, Paul J. Babicki Tabula Rosa Systems

Email response with no apparent relationship to the original email	**From:** Serkan Gecmen [Serkan@TabulaRosa.net] **Sent:** Tuesday, October 16, 2012 3:04 PM **To:** Paul Babicki **Subject:** RE: NetiquetteIQ Score Dear Paul: Where will you be next Tuesday, October 23? Thank you, Serkan Gecmen **From:** Paul Babicki [mailto:paul@TabulaRosa.net] **Sent:** Tuesday, October 16, 2012 2:16 PM **To:** Serkan Gecmen **Subject:** NetiquetteIQ Score Hello Serkan: Please send me my NetiquetteIQ rating. Thank you, Paul J. Babicki Tabula Rosa Systems

8. *Interim reply*—Often, one is not able to provide a full answer immediately. It is best to provide a temporary answer, such as "I am not sure but will find out as soon as possible and get back to you straight away." If the sender is confident that an answer can be provided on a certain time or date, he or she should state such in the message.

It would be appropriate to set up a calendar or other reminder when doing this. Strive to be accurate and predictable. If the sender is unable to provide an appropriate response, it is far better to state so.

9. *Forwarding*—Many of the rules of forwarding similarly apply to those composing or replying. The single most important action in forwarding is to ensure your content has been cleansed. Among the critical items to consider removing are

   A. Inappropriate content identifiers

   B. Irrelevant threads

    C. Confidential information such as finances, business transactions, address

    D. Personal information, social security number, passwords

    E. Expired items

    F. Nonstandard programs

    G. Anything the original author may object to

10. *Replying as an attachment*—How often does a would-be recipient say, "I did not receive the message" or "Please send me the last email you sent to my colleague"? It is perfectly reasonable and often desirable to send or forward an email as an attachment. One good reason is to preserve all of the content a correspondence may have. Another reason may be additional information and the validation of it. Finally, a person may have received a message that he or she was not able to open, and forwarding it as an attachment is required.

Angry replies

Before reacting in anger, consider some of the following points, and then take appropriate actions. Foremost, remember that an angry reply will seldom result in anything positive. The best approach is to consider the three Zs: namely, zero-tolerance reaction, zeal in replying, and Zen attitude and tone. To begin with, it is critical to understand what the cost of a flame war can be to all involved. A *flame war* is a term often used to describe email arguments that are unfriendly. Many escalate into increasingly intensive language or tone. The second consideration is creating zero tolerance toward situations or persons. This attitude may prove to have or cause far more loss than gain. The first step should be to pause and not reply rapidly, which will benefit both sides (more of a Zen approach, or the old count-to-ten approach).

By refraining from using zeal caused by anger, turn this instead into a situation where positives can occur. Consider the facts that prompted what is or appears to be an angry communication. Consideration should also be taken for any known or likely reasons that evoked an immediate negative reaction. Attempt also to visualize before sending a reply how to minimize any further irritation for everyone. When finally replying after a cooling-down session, ensure that, no matter what the outcome may be, matters are not made worse.

The above words (*The die is cast*) were spoken when Julius Caesar crossed the Rubicon. In his day, gambling with dice was very popular. The clearer meaning here is that once rolled, the dice result cannot be changed. One is better served to attempt to get clarification, inquiring in such a way as to seek further information, rather than to assume the worst. It is almost always best to ensure that no additional parties are brought into the communication, which could scarcely be of benefit for anyone involved and can only exacerbate the situation. Email flame-wars or multiple, back-and-forth, hostile email exchanges end up bringing in additional people, which makes it far more difficult to resolve what was started. Keep in mind that it is easier and less painful to resolve what may initially be simple or innocent misunderstandings.

> **"Alea jacta est."**
>
> - Julius Caesar

Sometimes, it may prove best not to respond to an angry email. This may provide a useful cooling-down interval and let a potentially time- consuming and damaging situation dissipate harmlessly. This situation can also contribute to increased anger from the original sender. There are several items to keep in mind when weighing this option of waiting. First, determine if a true question was asked or if an answer was asked for. Second, consideration should be given as to whether this is a personal, business, or necessary contact to maintain. Is the person or persons of significance to cause damage or continue a flame war with other common acquaintances? Perhaps the sender was bluffing or blowing off steam regarding a situation. Any of these considerations might have enough value to provide a logical reason to choose not to reply.

Finally, if one selects to reply, ensure that there is not a clouding of judgment. Take any steps, such as a delay of an hour or even a day, to provide for this. Consider also direct contact. The personal reaching out and contact may be just the solution. Additionally, make sure all reasonable considerations have been made to understand everyone's point of view. Realize that attempting to change another's opinion, philosophy, or feeling of being may be misunderstood.

If and when one does reply, one should keep true to the Zen of the three Zs. Senders should seek to appreciate and understand the position or condition that caused the situation. When objective reasoning is in place, then a reply can be created. Senders should also go over any important items step by step. Keep the text at a minimum, with proper attention given to tone, attitude, and normal Netiquette considerations. Ask if your reply is deemed satisfactory, or if it requires more information, and inquire if a further response is necessary.

If a determination has been made that an angry email sender is correct, it is essential to quickly reply and acknowledge what has been in error. If corrective action needs to be taken, good Netiquette is to clearly state what this is and provide a reasonable time line and explanation with all the particulars. If an apology is in order, it is important that it is done without delay. When this has been accomplished, a response for status is good Netiquette. If no response is given, one should not take offense. The recipient may believe the matter is closed. Lastly, decide if it is a reasonable action to inquire again, after an interval of at least several days, if all is in order. If no response again occurs, state that the matter will be considered closed if no further communication regarding this matter is tendered. At this point, it is best to let the matter rest.

Keeping templates

As is well known, more and more emails are being written and delivered by the day. Since the limits of Netiquette can often be strained from an individual's or company's policy, there are some actions to assist with catching up with email or avoiding mailbox backlog. One such method is to compose a series of templates. One example would be similar to an out-of-office automatic reply for business; another would be informal.

In essence, this process enables a user to have some time to catch up to accumulated messages and give the original sender due consideration.

Bad out-of-office example		I'm out of the office and on vacation. For urgent issues, please contact Jerry at support@trs.net or 888-123-4567. I'll address all other inquires when I return.
Good out-of-office example	Thank you for your message. I am currently out of the office with limited access to email. I will be returning on Friday, April 15. If you need assistance before then, you may reach me at 555-123-4567. For urgent issues, please contact Ralph at support@trs.net or 888-123-4567. Thank you, Gilbert Smith	

Some ideas for a template might be sales, peak season periods (e.g., April 15), or after major events. Some other popular reply templates might include the following:

1. Information request

2. Status request

3. Employment request

4. Directions or logistics

5. Long-term appointment or meeting

6. Multiple-part questions

7. Seasonal request

8. Confirmation of goods or services received

9. Referral to or for someone

10. Membership or subscription information

11. Request for quotation (RFQ)

As much as personalized templates can assist with replying to emails and maintain a good Netiquette flow, they should never be considered as a preferred form of communication with more important recipients.

Persistent emails

Certain individuals will continue to send emails regarding requests, open issues, or pending events. Some, in spite of direct and polite answers, continue to ask the same questions, which the recipient has promised to reply to when the answers are available. How should replies to these types of messages be addressed? Certainly, Netiquette almost always calls for reasonable replies to legitimate questions, both professional and personal.

Similar to the endless "Thank you," "You are welcome," "Goodbye," and "Best wishes" cycles, there does exist a limit when the cycle of emails should be stopped. After two or three replies that explain or promise a reply immediately when an answer is known or a situation becomes resolved, there is no longer an obligation to respond promptly. It is reasonable, after three of the same answers to the same question, that no further reply be given. The final answer might include a statement such as "asked and answered." When an update becomes known, or when the answer or resolution transpires, then the final reply can be given.

As always, special care and consideration should be extended to business situations, which cannot be compromised. Personal considerations can also be subject to a greater degree of patience.

Responding to rude email

When someone sends a rude or angry email, how should one respond? Here are possible options:

> **"Politeness works even with the rudest of people."**
>
> - I Ching

1. No reply

2. Change the subject/deflect

3. Polite but firm answer

4. Defer for a period of time

5. Agree but reply, stating that it might have been said better

6. Agree politely

Although it is usually best to pause before replying to impolite, terse, or insensitive emails, this delay should not be protracted. If the sender is a manager or a person of influence or authority, then a normal time to reply should not be delayed.

When not to respond

Certain emails do not warrant a response by Netiquette standards. It is still prudent to ensure a response is positively not required or may have some implications.

1. To a spam

2. After one thank-you (i.e., know when to stop)

3. When being provoked

4. To unsolicited messages with no specific relationship

5. To a Bcc other than the sender

6. If replying to a Bcc, do not use "reply to all"

7. Do not "reply to all" when no value is presented to all recipients

8. To out-of-the-office automated messages

9. When sender has set a noreply@***.com—this is done when the addressee is typically sending a message strictly for instruction purposes. Rather than leave the From field blank, which might cause a message to be ignored, placing this generic address in the From field encourages the addressee to read it. Usually the email will have information on making alternative contact.

Emails that lack closure

One of the premiere benefits derived from email is enabling the sender to quickly schedule, confirm, postpone, or cancel events. In addition, other situations of any kind can be introduced for the purpose of resolving any conflict or misunderstanding. However, too often emails result in generating ambiguity and multiple messages going back and forth. All participants in an email thread should avoid the following: "Let's speak tomorrow," "I will contact you later," "Give me a call mid-week," and "Maybe one day next week..."

Netiquette for wrongly addressed email

When email first began to be actively used, there was far more active use of Netiquette when emails were inadvertently sent or received. Since there were far fewer instances of malware, phishing, or criminal intent, the relative trust communicating with a stranger was far greater than in the current millennium. Users who received emails in error would often reply to the sender, informing him or her of the error. Of course, in today's environment, this is a rarity. There is good reason for ignoring email that has been wrongly delivered.

It is not bad Netiquette to ignore wrongly addressed email from a name or source that is unknown. The potential risks are too high. There may be extenuating circumstances to this policy. Here are several:

1. The email is meant for a person or group the recipient knows.

2. The email contains sensitive information.

3. The recipient is mistakenly cc'd from a known source.

4. The email is sent from a known sender but clearly intended for another.

If an email is mistakenly sent to someone and the recipient is known, it is the best Netiquette to immediately forward the mail to the intended party with a brief message, such as, "This clearly was intended for you and not me. The message was forwarded as soon as it was received."

When a completely unknown sender has incorrectly sent an email and it seems to contain important information, it is the best Netiquette to immediately delete the document, particularly in light of disclaimers being attached. Attachments should never be opened on these or any wrongly sent messages at any time.

Mistakenly sent emails often occur within an organization. The wrong group might be addressed, among many other factors. Again, this should be immediately acted upon by a reply to only the sender. It will be his or her responsibility to explain the situation to the intended recipient or group.

If someone wrongly receives an email from a known source outside of a company, it may very well be due to the wrong selection in an email contacts list. There also might have been a wrong selection from an email auto-complete application. Again, whatever the reason for the error, it is proper Netiquette to send a prompt email to the sender.

In any of the instances noted above, when replying, the proper way to do so is to attach the entire message in a new message. This provides the implication that the entire email, including any attachment, has been totally erased, and the sender's miscue has been fully cleared. It is also good Netiquette to erase the errant message and inform the person of the action.

It should be noted that if an email is sent in error, there is a record of such. When such an email is totally ignored, the sender may need to account at a later time for a failure to act on this situation in a responsible manner.

Chapter X - Sending, Resending, More Forwarding

Times to send (or not)

Netiquette's roots are in etiquette, social rules, and practices that find their origins in the most ancient societies. Because email is 24/7, the aspect of interval and timing can easily be compromised. Traditional correspondences were always limited by time for the services to deliver letters/calls/telegrams. The baby boomers generation was trained, in most households, to refrain from phone calls after certain evening hours and before certain morning hours. Letters, no matter when they were written, would arrive at the recipient's mailbox when the normal mail delivery completed its journey's cycle.

Because of email's capabilities to instantly deliver 24/7, someone can receive an email at 11:00 p.m., 2:00 a.m., or whenever the sender releases it. If the addressee receives email on a cell phone, there is a good possibility the device may be active, and a notification sound may awaken the person. Additionally, if the addressee is a manager or executive, the perception of someone emailing at 2:00 a.m. may be negative. Contrast this to someone sending at 6:00 a.m. This carries a far more positive impression: that is, of an early riser. So write away at any time, but send emails at reasonable times, preferably early morning (after 6:00 a.m.).

Another benefit of sending at optimal times is that emails that reach the destination inbox when the addressee is online have a far better likelihood of

1. being read

2. being read right away

3. receiving a rapid reply

Weekends and holidays

More and more people who access email do business or work on weekends and holidays. Does this practice have any effect upon those receiving emails? For personal correspondence, clearly there would rarely be a negative impact. These intervals may present the only times one might have to catch up on nonprofessional, family, or social activities. However, just as in sending professional emails at late hours may be bad Netiquette, doing so on holidays may have negative results. Many professionals have mechanisms that notify them when messages are received during nonworking hours or use a forwarding technology that alerts them.

It is best Netiquette to apply the same discretion when sending on weekends. It is very important not to use urgent flags or requests during these times as well unless there is due cause. To have someone feel he or she needs to respond to a message during off hours, and to later find out it wasn't necessary, can prove unfortunate.

International email

It has already been stated in these pages how instant communication can be properly used with correct Netiquette. This applies to international communications as well. Care and consideration should be given to the time windows. It cannot be expected for an overseas person to reply to a message that is received off hours to him or her but prime time in the United States. There are many time-zone references available online. If a message does need to be sent off hours, it is highly desirable for the sender to let the recipient know he or she (the sender) is aware of the difference, and, if a reply or action is anticipated, that an appropriate adjustment and/or expectation has been made.

Hyperbole

Weak or nonexistent subject lines have been discussed previously, in chapter I. Just as often, Netiquette is overlooked due to the overemphasized subject line that does not deliver

> **"The sky is falling!"**
>
> - Chicken Little

or correspond to some presumption in the content. Although it has been shown that some relevant or interesting subject line is needed, the wording or format can be as misleading as a weak or unrelated one is vague. Even though a more hyperbolic subject field may elicit a greater chance of being read, to do so consistently without merit may produce a dismissive reaction on future communications.

Similarly, the frequent use of excessive email program flags, such as red exclamation marks, will also usually produce the opposite of intended effects. When used properly, importance in subject fields or signifiers will be appreciated, welcomed, and read. Worst of all, the use of all uppercase letters, multiple exclamation marks, or all bold text in a subject field are all very poor Netiquette.

Unintended bait and switch

Just as in email promotions from many companies, an exaggerated subject line might completely differ from the intended target. Although this tactic may be deliberately used for spam marketing, it may less consciously be used with non-spam messages. One cause might be a lack of concentration in changing the subject line for the convenience of not having to open a new email template and completing the fields.

The reused template may also contain unintended urgent flags. The subject field might also contain previous multiple punctuation marks, all uppercase letters, or sensitive topics. There is rarely an instance to use a field in template and new "clean slate" formats should be used. The potential risks of not doing so are too high.

Sending templates

Just as with replying to emails with personalized templates (discussed in chapter IX), templates for sending can be proper Netiquette although not ideal. Their use is highly preferred to a mail-and-merge whenever possible. These messages are best for general mail where a recipient is not well known or likely may not be contacted again. Some examples of these are:

1. Thank-you for meeting, orders, interviews, and so on

2. Company hire

3. Survey or opinion

4. Reminder

5. Retirement/promotion/award

6. Seasonal event

7. Meeting schedule

8. Rejection of a bid, offer, or job request

9. Company announcement

10. Referral of a colleague or group.

Once again, it should be stressed that the best Netiquette for email is personalized as much as possible to maximize positive tone, ensure best results, and preserve positive relationships.

Fax to email

Although fax technology has greatly diminished in its use, faxes still are used for various situations and by entities that do not allow external web access. When situations occur in which fax-to-fax communication is not practical or possible, many utilities and services exist that allow bidirectional conversion; that is, fax to email or email to fax.

When a message is conveyed via this medium, normal Netiquette rules should be observed.

1. Verify the correct fax number.

2. Request permission to send to a fax.

3. Ask for a specific time to send a fax.

4. Do not send confidential information without permission.

5. Provide a full cover sheet with all information.

6. Ask for or provide immediate confirmation.

7. Mark appropriate faxes as confidential.

8. Do not send to multiple machines unless instructed.

9. Keep a record for when faxes were sent.

10. Do not use third-party machines for confidential faxes.

Partial listing of dangerous emails

The following categories represent common themes for email spammers and should be ignored.

False Emails	Virus Email Hoaxes	Giveaway Email Hoaxes	Charity Hoaxes
Bogus Warnings	Email Petitions and Protests	Email Chain Letters	Celebrity Email Hoaxes

Prank Emails	Bad Advice Emails	Funny Email Hoaxes	Unsubstantiated Emails
Missing Child Email Hoaxes	Phishing Scams	Nigerian Scams	Payment Transfer Job Scams
Email Lottery Scams	Miscellaneous Scams	Pharming Scams	Internet Dating Scams
Computer Security	Virus Information	Email Security	Spam Control

Three major credit bureaus

There are three major credit bureaus: Experian, TransUnion, and Equifax. Each is required to provide an individual's credit rating for free. Any email solicitation that deals with obtaining free scores should be ignored at all times.

Opt in and opt out

There is not a national opt-out registry similar to the Do Not Call for telephones. Services are available on many spam emails to opt out of junk mail. Users should never opt out if they didn't opt in. Many junk email options are the proper way to do this where unsolicited emails have "Opt Out" statements that typically require the recipient to respond via email to the originator. These promise to cease future spam from the originator. Some of these opt-out options are legitimate, while others might be phishing attempts to gain information for illegal purposes or to verify the email address is active. The latter situation is commonly referred to as harvesting. Additionally, a reply to an unsolicited email confirms that the ISP is not filtering spam.

Basically, opt-outs should be ignored unless the recipient positively knows that it is legitimate. Companies can also be contacted directly. There are also services available, many at no charge, to remove email addresses from groups such as credit card companies.

Replying to urgent or time-sensitive requests

An increasing amount of emails, in particular marketing ones, are being labeled or defined as urgent, time-sensitive, or of business urgency. Most recipients will give precedence to these marked messages. Unfortunately, the proliferation of these has numbed many into taking these for granted and not lending special attention to opening, reading, and taking appropriate action. Although it may be tempting to do so, ignoring the urgency of a message from a known sender is usually not in one's best interest.

Urgent emergencies

When an email proves indeed to be one that requires direct attention, then the appropriate response should be quickly given. If an action is required but it is not immediately possible to rectify the situation, an immediate answer should be provided, explaining the situation and when to expect the appropriate action. It is generally best to avoid details, excuses, or rationalizations. The sender should include, whenever possible, a realistic time range. Keep in mind it is far better to provide accurate and realistic promises than to have to repeat the process later.

Mildly important requests

If an urgently marked request is received, then proves to be essentially routine, it should be addressed appropriately (i.e., as a normal reply). As with any message, if an immediate fulfillment of a situation is not available, a proactive and realistic time should be conveyed as a reply. However, if the true urgency or significance does not exist, the resolution time can be longer.

Not-truly-urgent requests

When an urgently marked message proves not to be so, it is best to treat it as a normal message. Certain email senders will consistently overuse urgency flags. Rarely will any positive results come from bringing this subject up to the sender unless there is a high degree of certainty that any such comment or request will be accepted without some ill or hurt feelings. However, there are those exceptions, and many can be defined as follows:

1. The sender is employed by or reports to the recipient.

2. Direct damage has occurred based upon negative feedback from others, particularly in business interactions.

3. The sender's messages are being ignored.

4. The flagged message resulted in considerable cost or expenditure of resources when these were totally unnecessary.

5. The elevated situation caused other real priority situations to be ignored.

Some rules regarding replying to urgent requests

1. Be proactive to avoid critical email.

2. Maintain consistency in replies.

3. Follow Netiquette guidelines.

4. Keep promises.

5. Follow up on completed actions to verify that an "urgent" matter has been properly addressed.

6. Stay on target.

7. Keep messages brief.

8. If apologies are required, do so quickly.

9. Make sure of facts.

10. Keep "marked" messages and replies marked until all issues are resolved.

Auto-reply messages

Auto-reply as a tool has benefits, particularly for business, that are extremely useful. When a sender has a pressing need to reach a person or service and has no reply after a significant amount of time, this can lead to a number of different negative results. First, the sender may view the recipient as indifferent, indecisive, or incompetent. The long-term result might be negative in many other varied respects, such as financial loss, lack of confidence, or permanent loss of communication. Properly utilizing auto-reply can significantly eliminate most of the items stated above. When providing alternate sources of communication or contact, the creator of the auto-reply message must ensure that these sources are fully prepared to field any request and not ignore the potential person who will attempt to make contact.

When not to invoke auto-reply

1. With short absence from email access

2. When other resources are monitoring the recipient's email

3. If the email account is for casual use only

4. If messages can be monitored and addressed in a normal fashion

5. When an absence might invoke a negative connotation

Forwarding

When forwarding, it should be made certain that the email is being sent to the recipient's appropriate account (business, personal, group). If one chooses to send to a group, it should be ensured that this not going to cause any problems. It is best here to forward to individuals. Consideration should be given to using the Bcc method as well. Additionally, an explanation should be given to ensure a message or thread is being forwarded—and, if one is not the composer, to state a reason for the email.

Sometimes a message is returned because one of the recipients' addresses is typed incorrectly. Rather than resending the message again to everyone, it should be resent only to the addressee who did not receive it. One should make sure this is mentioned. One can accomplish this by forwarding the email as well. Similarly, with a successful resending to the recipients, explain what and why it is being done.

Resending messages

The resending method can be a very useful tool. Often a recipient has not received or has lost a message. If a message must be resent and include additional recipients, take the same care and steps as when forwarding. If the original email was a sender request, make sure to state, "second request" or "resent" in the Subject field.

Do not gloat about resending a message to prove a point, since the original meaning for sending a message may have been misread or misinterpreted by the sender. If a sender is resending a message that was not received, was lost, or needs more information, he or she should take proper care that the content is still timely, relevant, and complete. More information may need to be added, and, if this is the case, add the information separately and be clear as to how and why. Do not change the original message, since it may later be read or compared to the original.

Actions when an email is wrongly sent

Most email users have experienced the heart-sinking feeling in coming to the realization that an email was sent to the wrong person or group. The emotions can vary from mild embarrassment or irritation to full-scale panic. Similarly, ramifications might range from the wrongful recipient's not having a second thought to his or her being slightly annoyed to experiencing anger, resentment, or even taking action.

The following is an example of an email that shows how one error can cause great emotional distress and embarrassment to the sender.

On Friday, more than 1,300 employees of London-based Aviva Investors walked into their offices, strolled over to their desks, booted up their computers, and checked their emails, only to learn the shocking news: They would be leaving the company. The email ordered them to hand over company property and security passes before leaving the building, and left the staff with one final line: "I would like to take this opportunity to thank you and wish you all the best for the future." This email was sent to Aviva's worldwide staff of 1,300 people, with bases in the US, UK, France, Spain, Sweden, Canada, Italy, Ireland, Germany, Norway, Poland, Switzerland, Belgium, Austria, Finland, and the Netherlands. And it was all one giant mistake: The email was intended for only one individual.

What actions should be taken? Some email programs allow for message recall, but this rarely works even if done quickly. In all instances, a brief email should be sent acknowledging the mistake and making assurances, not excuses, that more care will be provided in the future. If the potential fallout from the error may cause serious results, such as job loss or financial repercussions, then a more detailed email (or personal communication via phone or face to face) might be better served. If certain damage has been done, financial or otherwise, the sender should ask the recipient to suggest a satisfactory solution. Clearly, the actions to be taken with the example shown above are to set the matter straight and issue an immediate apology.

Another necessary action that should be taken immediately after a wrongly sent email is to make sure the true, intended recipient is sent the errant correspondence. Of course, it is an essential aspect of Netiquette to explain the error, how it happened, and what, if anything, was the corrective action. There should also be a request to acknowledge receipt of the email.

Actions when an email with multiple addressees is returned because of one recipient's delivery error

On those occasions when an email is sent to more than one person and a failure occurs for only one of the intended recipients, there are different actions the sender selects. One is simply to resend the message after correcting any possible mistakes in the rejected email address. This can be awkward, since the other addressees will have two identical emails.

If this approach is taken, either a resend comment should be appended to the description field noting the repetition or another approach that some senders choose is to resend the message only to the person who did not receive it. Although this does prevent duplicate emails to the other recipients, the single addressee will not have the knowledge of the others who have the same email. This is because the receiver does not see the original Cc list of names. This can cause miscommunication, possible confusion, or some embarrassment.

Resending a returned email

To correct this situation, the sender needs to inform the recipient of what occurred and who else received the email. This should be done in the first sentence.

The third and best Netiquette method in resending the single email is simply to forward it from the sent box with a brief note on the description line or as the first sentence. This will prevent most errors or misunderstandings.

Chapter XI - Elements of a Business Email

> "A slip of a foot you may soon recover, but a slip of the tongue you may never get over."
>
> - Benjamin Franklin

There is no category of email where Netiquette is more important than business email. Adherence to Netiquette assumes following epolicy rules and guidelines of companies by employees. Additionally, laws, such as the Electronic Communication Privacy Act, are core to proper Netiquette as well as legal behavior. Netiquette in business necessitates more formalities and stricter guidelines with fewer popular types of email usage. This would include items such as emoticons, abbreviations, and acronyms. Most business Netiquette adheres to traditional elements, formats, styles, and grammar used long before the Internet and email existed. Arguably, the core of appropriate business email is proper content.

Business email content

One single email can create huge damage to a company or to an organization. This could be in the form of damage to finances, reputation, or intellectual property, or even legal punishment. Employers are responsible for the behavior of their employees. To minimize the potential damage by employees, organizations use disclaimers. The basic types of disclaimers for company outbound email are as follows:

1. Confidentiality

2. Malware

3. Employer liability

4. Contract negotiation

5. Negligent misstatement

6. Complete disclaimer

7. Compliance disclaimer

8. Department disclaimer

These are the very basic types of disclaimer and the core of any epolicy. Many disclaimers take on a threatening tone, such as the negligent misstatement example listed later in this chapter. To really achieve compliance when publishing these statements, a more polite tone is encouraged, such as the one below. A sample of one of these would be as follows:

Breach of Confidentiality and Accidental Breach of Confidentiality

This email and any files transmitted with it are confidential and intended solely for the use of the individual or entity to whom they are addressed. If you have received this email in error, please notify the system manager. If you are not the named addressee, you should not disseminate, distribute, or copy this email. Please notify the sender immediately by email if you have received this email by mistake and delete this email from your system.

Virus warning

Any outbound email should be scanned/scrubbed for viruses and malware. Best efforts and diligence may not always be 100 percent. Since a sender can arguably be liable for damage by malware or suffer from loss of reputation, many companies will have a disclaimer for this. Even certain individual private correspondence of a nonbusiness nature can have a disclaimer. It may appear strange or ominous in certain situations and is at the discretion of the individual to provide one if it is believed this serves his or her interest to do so. It would not be appropriate to send a disclaimer for an interview cover letter.

One example of a malware disclaimer would be as follows:

Transmission of Malware

WARNING: Viruses and damaging programs can be delivered through email. The recipient should check all email and any attachments for the presence of viruses and malware. This sender accepts no liability for any damage caused by any virus transmitted by this email. This organization cannot be guaranteed to be secure or error-free, as information could be intercepted or contain viruses. The sender, therefore, does not accept liability for any errors or omissions in the contents of this message that arise as a result of email transmission.

Employer liability

This disclaimer is often used when there is a heavy volume of outbound email related to dissemination of information related to consulting, sales, advice, or opinion. A sample of this type of disclaimer follows:

Any views or opinions presented in this email are solely those of the author and do not necessarily represent those of this company or any of its affiliates. Employees of this company are expressly required to refrain from making defamatory statements and not to infringe or authorize any infringement of copyright or any other legal right by email communications. Any such communication is contrary to organizational policy and outside the scope of the employment of the individual responsible. The company will not accept any liability in respect of such communication, and the employee responsible will be personally liable for any damages or other liability arising.

Contracts

If any organization is significantly engaged in contracts where the process involves written agreements, a disclaimer may include some of the following verbiage.

No employee or agent is authorized to conclude any binding agreement on behalf of this company with another party by email without express written confirmation by an authorized company officer.

Negligence on statements

This is a straightforward protection where a relatively minor or unintentional (even in tone) statement or disclosure is made. This style may be more desirable than lengthy statements. The following can be added to for any needed detail:

Negligent Misstatement

Our organization accepts no liability for the content of this email or for the results of any actions taken on the basis of the information given, unless that information is subsequently confirmed separately in writing. If you are not the intended recipient, you are notified that disclosing, copying, distributing, or taking any action on the contents of this information is strictly prohibited.

Full disclosure

The following incorporates a full range of issues:

Complete Disclaimers

This message contains confidential information. If you are not the named addressee, you should not disseminate, distribute, or copy this email. Please notify the sender immediately by email if you have received this email by mistake, and delete this email from your system. Email transmission cannot be guaranteed to be secure or error-free, as information could be intercepted, corrupted, lost, destroyed, arrive late, incomplete, or contain viruses. The sender, therefore, does not accept liability for any errors or omissions in the contents of this message that arises as a result of email transmission. If verification is required, please request a hard-copy version.

Compliance disclaimers

These statements will most often be related to an industry and its respective government rules and regulations, such as HIPPA and healthcare. Here is such a sample:

> Information contained in this document represents the NC DHHA HIPAA Program Management Office (PMO) staff's views and interpretations of HIPAA. This information is subject to change and should be used only for the purpose intended by the NC DHHS HIPSS PMO. If you believe that information obtained from this document is inaccurate or out-of-date, please notify the DHHS HIPSS PMO via email.

Department disclaimers

Many larger organizations choose to implement disclaimer statements for intra-company email. These would typically be departments of finance, IT, research, marketing, and the board of directors. Samples of these are readily available online or in published format.

The purpose of presenting these disclaimers is to stress good Netiquette to be effective in properly sending and replying to businesses. It is important to use proper language, content, and care to ensure optimal and error-free email correspondence.

> This transmitted file is confidential to the department and to the group or individual they are addressed to. If you have received this message in error, please refer it to the system manager.

Familiarity in email correspondence

Extended business correspondence or interaction might become friendlier and less formal over time. These business friendships lend themselves to bits of personal information being exchanged. Such relationships and the knowledge they bring can be very useful in building rapport, trust, and better business success. Netiquette certainly includes asking and conveying niceties, some more specific than others. Emails conveying a good balance are preferable and typically more effective.

There are inherent pitfalls in writing about personal topics. One of the most obvious of these is depicting personal information not known to other recipients, some of whom may be total strangers. Another drawback is that any third party might be uncomfortable, or deem unprofessional, having anything but business tone and content. Yet one further drawback to conveyance of personal information is "too much information," where the personal content overshadows the business at hand.

Care should be taken to minimize personal small talk when topics are in an emergency or crisis mode as well, for such chitchat may be viewed as deflecting or minimizing the real purpose of the communication. The same holds true for topics such as financial negotiations, and legal, medical, or job emails. Once more serious conditions are removed or settled, it is far more appropriate to continue with a better-balanced tone and content. Essentially, the more serious or complex the central issue, the less time and attention should be given to personal or peripheral information.

Employment email Netiquette

Comprehensive books and articles have been written pertaining to all aspects of employment emails. Recruitment, résumé submission, follow-up to interviews, acceptance/rejection of offers, and even terminations are among the most important types of emails you can compose or receive, yet a very large segment of these is lacking some of the most basic aspects of Netiquette discussed throughout this book.

Job recruitment

There are both obvious and less evident practices of Netiquette to follow for a recruiter. If the recruiter is a third party for an employer, there is a responsibility for acting on behalf of a hiring person or company. Since the recruiter also has communication with the job seeker, there should be appropriate Netiquette to this person as well. Many job-recruiting emails are written as mail merge letters, totally lacking formatting, tone, significant content, and especially personalization. Clearly, if a recruiter is seeking qualified prospective employees, the presence of Netiquette in correspondence, from basic solicitation through to qualification and employment offers, is vital. In highly competitive markets, even the slightest lack of positive, respectful, or personalized content can lead to failure of the desired results.

When initiating a correspondence, the recipient will generally be from the following categories: unknown or "cold," previously contacted or encountered, or qualified and vetted within or outside the organization. Although much personalization with an unknown is not usually possible, following the basic rules of Netiquette is essential. These would include the mail identification fields and a proper and descriptive subject line as well as a salutation with a name. The recruiter should always send correspondence to a personal account. The initial paragraph should include an introduction, purpose, and explanation of how the addressee has been identified. The next segment might have any combination of various kinds of information—for example, an opportunity description, a specific situation, or a lead-in, such as a recommendation.

Many recruiters dangle attractive opportunities to potential prospects. This is sometimes knowingly done without a real, concrete job available, usually to obtain a client. Such a methodology is simply not in keeping with Netiquette, ethics, or productive activity.

Common forms of business communications

1. Business to business

2. Business to customer

3. Marketing

4. Invitations

5. Introductions

6. Cover—résumé

7. Thank you

8. Newsletter

9. Complaints

10. Solicitation

11. Employment--offer/acceptance/decline

12. Scheduling

13. Memorandum of understanding (MOU)

14. Cover—proposal

15. Reference

16. Billing

17. Promotion

18. Letter of credit

19. Receipt of the email/attachment

20. Nondisclosure

Chapter XII - Attachments

> **"Getting information off the Internet is like taking a drink from a fire hydrant."**
>
> - Mitchell Kapor

Using attachments greatly enhances the capabilities and even potential hazards of email. Due to the significant differences and compatibilities of different mail programs, many attached items—such as tables, charts, documents with advanced formatting, and items that require or demand editing integrity—are critical to communication dynamics. Nonetheless, many obstacles and potential for problems exist when using attachments. What follows are examples where attachments can manifest poor results and loss of productivity or worse.

In the earliest days of email, a limited number of formats existed. However, the rapid proliferation of programs has produced hundreds, if not thousands, of formats. These are identified by their file extensions (e.g., .txt, .pdf). A considerable listing of these is provided in Appendix H. Although many programs can read multiple formats, these are no universal file readers. It follows that to read these attachments, the native program must be installed.

The sender must take care to ensure that the recipients can easily open an attachment, particularly an important or critical one. This is, of course, crucial in business communication and less so in personal email. Nonetheless, it may take a significant amount of time to open an attachment that might have been intended for quick review or action. Often, once a new program is installed, it may take the user some time to negotiate or operate the program. If this fails, the attachment may never be opened.

For many, attachment size is not a problem. For many others, the size of an attached file is a consideration, as it may have even a greater negative effect than a file attribute or format. Many Internet service providers (ISPs) have limitation for file size or mailbox size. Large files (5 MB or more) can be rejected altogether, or they may exhaust allotment of mailbox capacity. Thus, a recipient may not even know a message was sent and rejected. Large attachments, even when accepted, might fill the recipient's mailbox, which will result in disruption of service. Finally, small laptops or most smartphones could have performance issues when attachments are opened. There are several ways to avoid the pitfalls of attachment size. The first is to be selective when sending large files or multiple smaller ones. In the former case, many files can be significantly reduced by file compression programs, of which there are many. At least one of the popular ones is resident on most desktops or laptops. If other formats for document size reduction are appropriate, such as .pdf, this is a very good approach. In the case of the latter--multiple-attachment email--simply sending multiple messages with fewer attachments per email is practical, straightforward, and sure to reduce or eliminate the stress of unwieldy attachments.

Potential hazards of attachments

Most attachments are simply a means of document delivery. However, it has also become commonplace for hackers to use attachments to launch cyber-attacks, typically with executable code, which produce many varied effects, some highly destructive and malicious. When a recipient receives a suspicious attachment, it should be scanned and, unless it is from a trusted source, not opened. Some corporations, hosting companies, and ISPs will block, quarantine, or remove files with specifically identified file extensions. It is beneficial to consider at least some of these security measures to prevent inadvertent file removal. Care should be taken as well not to forward such messages without a security scan.

1. Do not send attachments that are not needed.

2. Do not return attachments when replying. The original sender knows what he or she attached.

Finally, when attachments are sent, some may have similar names to other files on the sender's system. With an inadvertent slip, the wrong attachment may go out, perhaps a compromising or confidential document. Therefore, opening attachments to validate they are appropriate and correct is critical to a proper email process.

Titles of attachments are often visible in a mailbox preview mode. These titles can be very important for a number of reasons. Primarily, an accurate and appropriately named attachment will encourage the recipient to open the email and read the attachment. If an attachment is not appropriately named, opening it may be delayed or dropped altogether. Some important considerations to use in titling attachments are date and specific content (e.g., proposal, invoice, résumé, or author). Avoid using titles that are very long, contain all numeric characters, do not represent the content, or have inappropriate information. The last might contain dates long since past or very generic names such as "letter," "schedule," and so forth. Maintaining a structured process such as consecutive numbering or defining categories is not only useful for the recipient but also for the sender. It is also important to adhere to Netiquette in attachment titles by using correct punctuation, capitalization, and spelling.

Metadata and drafts in attachments

Certain programs can actively send all of the corrections already visible. Some programs leave hidden information, or metadata, which can be retrieved. Care should be given to prevent this, as it may lead to lawsuits, security breaches, or other negative situations. Attention should be given to "clean" these files or use an attachment format that will erase the metadata. Even better, converting attachments to a .pdf or other unchangeable file format eliminates this danger.

Dos for attachments	**Don'ts** for attachments
• Be consistent with names or descriptions	• Have too few or too many characters
• Verify an attachment need	• Send "v" card attachments unless requested
• Capitalize the title	• Reply to someone with the attachment he or she sent you
• "Zip" or compress large files	• Send attachments with possible compromising metadata
• Use universal formats	
• Clean metadata	
• Title attachments for convenience in storage	

Mail To links

The Mail To link should not be confused with a hyperlink. This type of link provides a shortcut to allow a user to automatically launch an email template with a minimum of an addressee form filled in. However, more information can be provided, which can include subject line data, Cc recipients, or even text.

Mail To links are most often used in email signatures (see chapter II) but they can be placed anywhere within a message. When doing this, the same Netiquette usage should be followed, explaining what the link is, how to use it, and where or how it might fail. There are few email programs that no longer support or provide the capability to create a Mail To link. One example of this is plain text format.

There are also security issues where security settings may block or cause a prompt to appear before any message can be sent. Many users may be prone to cancel the operation from a lack of knowledge or inadvertently wrong response.

Where to place links in email

www.NetiquetteIQ.com + Enter will produce: www.NetiquetteIQ.com with most programs. Wether entering a ".com" address and hitting Enter will establish a hyperlink or not depends on individual mail programs and their default or chosen preferences.

Links should be tested for accuracy before the document is sent. This is critical and represents the equivalent of a spell-check—all links within a message should be properly described prior to the link itself: "Please see the website of NetiquetteIQ.com to take a free email IQ test."

Avoid placing a URL or link within the subject field. This is due to several reasons. The first is that the text of the link may not yet be an active hyperlink. The second is the link will sometimes need to be moved. Additionally, there is no direct way to explain what the link is for. Lastly, the email recipient may not open the mail, since the description has been taken up by the link itself.

As stated above, most email products now support links. These items are typical websites. An Internet link or hyperlink is text coded to provide direct access to a website and specifically intended to assist a user. These links are usually distinguished by a different font attribute, such as a different color. One sample of direct link to a website is [www. NetiquetteIQ.com]. If coded, when this is clicked, the link will connect the user to the website cited.

Often, it is necessary to provide a web link within a message. This might be for the purpose of directing the recipient to a site or page for information. When placing a link within the document, there are several procedures to convey proper Netiquette and clarity. Any web link or hyperlink should be identified clearly and placed on an individual link to reduce the possibility of truncation and minimize any break in the link. When entering a website URL or link manually within an email, the entry should immediately be followed by a carriage return or hitting the Enter key to activate the link.

Placing images within an email

Typically, correct Netiquette assumes a minimization of graphs, photos, or animations within an email (see chapter II). There are numerous reasons for this. However, there may be occasions for items to be inserted directly. Examples of these situations are often personal, such as birthdays, holidays, or personal signatures. Background images, newsletters, and logos can be used at certain times or in certain circumstances. When such situations as described above do exist, then a few considerations should be given to ensure proper Netiquette:

1. Sizing should be reasonably minimized

2. Capability of forwarding may be limited

3. Possible security concerns (i.e., being filtered) should be addressed. Filtering in email is a method of checking all data in a correspondence and removing suspicious content based on rules such as words that are likely to be in spam or viruses.

4. Recipient's support of the format

5. Minimization of overdesign

Some definitions

URI	Uniform resource identifier
URL	Uniform reform resource locator, web address
Web link	Text to activate an Internet site
Hyperlink	A "direction" to another location or file
Web address	The address of a website

Chapter XIII - Legal Issues

> **"My original response was to sue her for defamation of character but then I realized I had no character."**
>
> - Charles Barkley

Books, articles, and papers have long been covered by copyright protection. Email is also considered to have copyright protection but by its very nature opens the door to more extensive and common abuse. Since email is a form of electronic media, it can be massively distributed, forwarded, duplicated, and posted. Since it is a creative work—a medium of expression—the sender retains the copyright interest in anything he or she sends. For example, if a person sends someone an email that is copied, the email is pulled down from a server, saved, and then pasted elsewhere. If this is done without permission, it is not legal.

However, there is a general consensus that the above does not apply when posting on the Internet. By sending a person an email, the sender has no reason to assume that it is going to be posted on the receiver's site. Therefore, most likely, the implied license will not cover that. To clarify, an email recipient does not have an inherent right to copy or post an email. Those issues have to be taken case by case. Here is a brief overview of the differences among patents, trademarks, and copyrights. A patent is a tangible manifestation of an idea and not the idea alone. This can be the NetiquetteIQ test. (See www.netiquetteIQ. com.) A trademark is a symbol, often a logo of a product. See the NetiquetteIQ logo on this book's cover. A copyright is the expression of an idea through a medium such as NetiquetteIQ software.

Email privacy

The privacy issue is much more complex than issues of copyright and, unfortunately, cannot be completely answered here. The right to privacy greatly depends upon five things:

1. The laws of the state(s) involved

2. What was in the email

3. What information was posted

4. Whether or not the person who sent the email is a public figure

5. The illegality potential

One certainty here is that a person who thrusts him- or herself into the public spotlight—for example, by running a site or introducing him- or herself into a major controversy—has fewer privacy protections than a regular citizen. This is not to say it would not be a privacy violation to post something from a public figure; it would just be a harder privacy case to make. The real issue is what is in the email and what is posted. If it is a rave review for a restaurant, that is much different than posting a secret about someone.

Defamation

Defamation is easier to do with email than through other mediums. If you quote someone from an email but only with select certain portions that change the meaning of what is said or distort the content, it can be a strong case for defamation. If you do not put the quote into context, and it besmirches someone's reputation, that can also be considered defamation. If someone does it to you, there are many potential avenues of attack and several ways it is actionable in court. Still, if you are worried about email privacy, put a disclaimer in your footer indicating that the email is considered private and is not for publication (see chapter XI). It really is not necessary for the most part but is never a bad idea.

If an email is forwarded and part of it is changed or left out with a negative result or changed meaning, it is defamation.

For Example: *The governor and his party proposed a very popular bill for cutting taxes, one of his campaign promises. When the document was sent to the legislature, the opposing party added a significant amount of partisan riders that would cut popular programs. Upon reading the measure, the governor commented, "The legislature has passed the bill. In its current form, I have decided to veto it and send it back, even though it was a campaign promise. When the bill is restored to its original form, I will gladly sign it."*

If the last sentence is removed, it will change the entire context of the quote.

When good Netiquette is practiced, defamation, bullying, libel, and slander will occur less frequently. Defamation of character is written or spoken injury to a person or organization's reputation. Libel is the written act of defamation. Slander is the verbal act of defamation. Malice means intent to do harm.

What defamation is not

Generally, a statement made about an indefinable group of people or organizations cannot be defamation. Take "lawyers are crooks," for example; there is no name or clearly defined victim. However, "John Law Firm is a crooked practice" indisputably defines a victim. The definition of defamation is "the speaking of slanderous words of a person so as, de bona fama aliquid detrahere, to hurt his good name."

Incorrect assumptions about email ownership

Many younger email/Internet users have seldom or never experienced doing research from traditional sources such as books, maga-

zines, or newspapers. Older email/Internet users who have had experience with non-electronic forms of information were most often taught
about plagiarism, copying, or otherwise misusing information and
writing not their own. Both of the aforementioned groups carry assumptions regarding ownership based upon many dynamics by and
from which electronic data and capabilities have changed traditional
values.

The following are some common practices many users from all
demographic groups have misconceptions about and wrongfully use
without any thought of possible wrongdoing.

1. *The use of someone's email or work with acknowledgment of an author's name and data location is permissible.* Wrong: permission is
necessary.

2. *Blocks of text, photos, or email can be cut and pasted into someone
else's email, blog, or other content.* Wrong: this is still another's content.

3. *Ownership of Internet email content created by another for marketing, newsletters, or announcements is automatically given to the
contractor.* Not correct: ownership is not automatically carried
over unless contractually agreed to.

4. *Emails sent to companies, groups, or individuals that express sentiment or provide suggestions or information can be posted freely.* Incorrect: ownership of the content is the author's, and permission
must be given.

5. *Display of email or images from other sites is permissible when
showing a specific relationship.* Incorrect: Permission must be ob-
tained from the owner.

The instances noted above are examples of inadvertent Netiquette
abuse, specifically plagiarism. In traditional situations, these situations
probably would not happen. Indeed, these occurrences reflect the importance of Netiquette education.

Email privacy--specific legal references

As long as there is email, there will be questions concerning its privacy. The origins of the Fourth Amendment date back to circa 1754, when British tax collectors were given the powers to search homes and private records of colonists. It is this amendment that guarantees privacy. There are a number of laws that have been enacted specifically to provide clarity and protection given by this original law. To discuss them in detail is not in the scope of this book, but some summarizations will be stated in this section.

The Electronic Communications Privacy Act (ECPA) was enacted in 1986 to define federal electronic eavesdropping provisions. It was intended to create "a fair balance between the privacy expectations of citizens and the legitimate needs of law enforcement." Congress also sought to address new technologies by assuring that personal information would remain safe.

The following table constitutes the legal actions that are needed to access the contents of an email at various times as outlined by epic.org.

> "The right of the people to be secure in their persons, houses, papers and effects, against unreasonable searches and seizures, shall not be violated, and no Warrants shall issue, but upon probable cause, supported by Oath or affirmation, and particularly describing the place to be searched, and the persons or things to be seized."
>
> - Fourth Amendment of the Constitution of the United States

Type of Communication	Required for Law Enforcement Access	Statute
Email in transit	Warrant	18 U.S.C.§ 2516
Email in storage on home computer	Warrant	4th Amendment, US Constitution
Email in remote storage, opened	Subpoena	18 U.S.C.§ 2703
Email in remote storage, unopened, stored for 180 days or less	Warrant	18 U.S.C.§ 2703
Email in remote storage, unopened, stored for more than 180 days	Subpoena	18 U.S.C.§ 2703

In addition to the specific government exceptions outline above, there is other information that the government is empowered to collect from communications providers in the form of customer records. Under § 2703, an administrative subpoena—a National Security Letter (NSL)—can be served on a company to compel it to disclose basic subscriber information. Section 2703 also allows a court to issue an order for records; whether an NSL or court order is warranted depends upon the information that is sought.

Pen registers and trap-and-trace

Pen registers and trap-and-trace devices provide only the origin and destination of email and other communications. The Supreme Court has held that there is no reasonable expectation of privacy of this information, because the service provider has access to it. The company must use this information to ensure communications are properly delivered. The Pen-Register Act covers pen registers/trap-and-trace. Because email subject lines contain content, their use on emails, per revision in the USA Patriot Act, must include the sender and addressee but not necessarily the subject. IP addresses and port numbers associated with the communication are not exempted by the act. The Pen-Register Act specifically applies to hardware that captures content. ECPA generally prohibits the installation or use of any device that serves as a pen register or trap-and-trace. Amendments in the USA Patriot Act encompass software as well.

ECPA provides guidelines for law enforcement to access data: with the Stored Communications Act, the government is able to access specific stored communications without a warrant.

Prohibition on access of communications

The Stored Communications Act addresses access to stored communications. This primarily refers to emails that are not in transit. The Act makes it unlawful to access a facility in which electronic communication services are provided and obtain, alter, or prevent unauthorized access to electronic communication while it is in electronic storage in a system.

Intercepting email

Storing and accessing email is easier than ever for employers. The Electronic Communications Privacy Act (ECPA) of 1986 prohibits the intentional interception of "any wire, oral, or electronic communication." However, it does include a business-use exemption that permits email monitoring. This law often comes under challenge and includes several components where, if an employee is using a company-owned computer and an employer can show a valid business reason for monitoring that employee's email, then the employer is well within his or her rights to do so. Moreover, if employees have consented to email monitoring, then a company can monitor their calls or emails.

The ECPA differentiates between business email content, which may be monitored, and personal emails, which are private. For the sender of email, it is clear that personal information should not be sent through business or non-secure accounts.

Social email privacy

An ongoing area of debate is email privacy. The following are considerations pertaining to policies and laws in this area. The media often comments about companies' asking job candidates for their Facebook passwords as part of the employment screening process. There is no federal law prohibiting this. The Department of Justice, however, considers it a crime to ask an employee or candidate for access. Both are in direct violation of Facebook's Terms of Service, which state, "You will not solicit login information or access an account belonging to someone else… You will not share your password…let anyone else access your account, or do anything else that might jeopardize the security of your account." Many states are now looking to make this practice illegal. Asking for personal passwords is a clear privacy violation and is unethical. Employers must not access profile information to determine an employee's religious, sexual, or political views. Because email and social media go hand-in-hand, this section is included in this book.

Chapter XIV - Special Occasions

> **"Act as if what you do makes a difference. It does."**
>
> - William James

> **"Be kind whenever possible. It is always possible."**
>
> - Dalai Lama

Netiquette for Special Occasions Categories

Generic business emails have been discussed previously. More specifically, there are categories that bear individual discussion regarding the appropriate Netiquette. In the context of these, they are most typically open and general knowledge. To broadcast these in an internal company broadcast is a very nice way to provide positive praise to the individual and any relevant people and associates. Care should be given to ensure privacy, timeliness, and relevancy.

Retirement announcement by company

Similar to promotional email, care and attention should be given to focus on relevant public details. Jokes are best omitted. Too much information and details that may prove detrimental outside of the company should not be given.

Retirement announcement by employee

Economic conditions and uncertainty have changed the pattern of retirements. There are arguably far more incentivized and forced retirements than ever. Whatever the circumstances, employee-announced retirement should be far more limited in distribution, confidential detail, and emotion: basically, Netiquette at its best. It should be remembered that anything written in the context of retirement will be on permanent record, susceptible to being forwarded or shared without permission, and possibly critically scrutinized for content, tone, and potentially damaging information. If a retiree wants to notify fellow employees of retirement, this is best done offline but with the same caution stated in the previous paragraph. Resentment and negative emotions toward a former employer should not be presented via email.

Ecards

Email has rapidly fostered a growing trend to replace special-occasion communications with electronic ones. Ecards are now available for all holidays, personal milestones, social events, and public announcements. Just as with any personal communication, a significant part of content is diluted or removed when email is involved. As described in other chapters, body language, tone, and parts of interpersonal contact are eliminated or experienced differently.

Proper Netiquette for ecards should be practiced and maintained with the same standards of vigilance and discipline to ensure that the desired result of the communication is maximized. Whereby much direct contact, mail, or letters can be replaced by email to some extent, there is a further diminishing value when ecards or their variants are used. Forms of ecards are available as readily as paper cards in the display racks of stationary stores. These can, for the most part, be serious, humorous, or witty, as the following list shows:

Business
Promotion
Retirement by employer
Firing

Graduation
All levels

Announcements
New Employee
Tributes
Promotions

Engagements

Obituaries
Notifications

Major Losses
Relatives

Anniversary
Marriage
Work

Religious
Baptism
All Denominations

Holidays
Valentine
Halloween
St Patrick's Day
All Nationalities

Parties
Invitations
Cyber Parties

Mother's /Father's Day

Birthdays
Child
Adult
Family
Coworker
Customer
    Milestone

Get Well
Serious
Humorous

Relationship
Separation

Cartoons
Political from strips

Thank You
All occasions

One should note that many ecards are free, but some of these point to advertisements. This may not be the image one would like to show.

Holiday email

Email and ecards are increasingly being used by businesses, acquaintances, and family to extend greetings to others. Many ecards or email companies offer an unlimited selection of design and templates, not only for national and personal holidays but also for international ones. The following sections discuss key Netiquette issues for businesses regarding birthdays and holidays.

Business birthdays

Many businesses send birthday messages to their customers or internal employees. These are typically boilerplate in nature and contain basic good wishes. Proper Netiquette calls for ensuring that there is no ill humor, mention of age, or personal information.

Personal birthdays

These emails or ecards differ vastly from their business counterparts. Most of the Netiquette that is demanded with these messages is basic, conventional Netiquette. Email birthday messages should most often be sent only to the birthday person. Items such as age or potentially sensitive issues should be avoided. There are increasing numbers of "virtual parties" being conducted, which have taken advantage of collaboration software or groupware sites. These parties have decorations, games, virtual food, even presents that can be presented virtually. Invitations should be done via email or with evites.

Other religious and holiday email and ecards

Most global holidays are little known outside of their respective religions or countries, so care and requisite Netiquette should be taken to ensure delivering appropriate and timely messages. In order to ensure this, ecards are probably the most prudent approach, and they are readily available through many online sources when a more personal contact is desired. Here are some dos and don'ts to be mindful of:

Dos	Don'ts
• Understand if a holiday is a festive one or a solemn one	• Use the ecard or email for other items
• Be timely and accurate	• Copy too many addresses
• Be brief	• Use slang

- Spell-check, especially names and holidays
- Rely strictly on spell-checks—most are American
- Compare to one's own personal holidays

Email Condolences

Sympathies and condolences are the most sensitive emails. Typically, these should not be used, unless there are significant distances, logistic difficulties, or time constraints. Additionally, there should be an existing comfort or established pattern of communicating with the intended recipient.

Dos	Don'ts
• Name the person	• Discuss negatives
• Offer your thoughts	• Rationalize with clichés such as "for the best"
• Present a compliment or pleasant recollection	• Change the subject or digress
• Ask to pass along the condolences to others	• Exceed more than a few sentences
• Offer assistance and state how/where you can be reached	• Mention money

Resignations

It is perhaps best to provide a resignation by regular mail. This situation is one of the most sensitive email categories. Many resignations are not expected nor well received. Others have accentuated emotional overtones. Therefore, it is best to maintain brevity and ensure that only basic information is given. This data should include the current date, the effective notice time, and a short thank-you with an offer to facilitate any issues during the transition time. Obviously, the normal salutation, signature, and contact information are necessarily included as well.

As has been stated elsewhere, brevity is best. Any additional information, such as the next employer, should be excluded. If there are benefits, expenses, accrued vacation, or entitlements that are outstanding, any or all should be addressed. Finally, an acknowledgment from the employer should be requested, with the proper place to email or mail by postal service.

Employer acceptance of employee resignation

It is both appropriate Netiquette and good business practice to acknowledge an employee's resignation. Although this process would be best served by postal mail, there are instances that may necessitate an email or both an email and postal letter. This may be because of time constraints, emergencies, or logistical situations.

Because this type of correspondence may be a final communication, all appropriate information should be included. Proper Netiquette should be maintained to avoid any adverse actions by the former employee. All responsibilities expected of the employee should be stated, together with special requests. If formal postal communication is to follow, this should be noted as well.

Security issues with ecards

One of the major downsides of ecards is that security can be compromised: when someone purchases an ecard, he or she is providing information to the seller, or third party. One of the more extreme examples of this is that the Children's Online Privacy Protection Act (COPPA) is suspended to allow sites to accept a child's ecard request and addresses without parental permission, as would normally be the case. There are also countless scams involving ecards, which can mislead children or people of any age. It is almost too much to ask certain people to have the discipline not to open ecards.

For those who will steadfastly refuse to open an ecard, there may very well be times when a legitimate message goes unopened—still another negative outcome. This can end up with an effect such as having the recipient feel disappointment that he or she did not receive a greeting or invitation by someone he or she was expecting to hear from.

While there is much positive impact associated with ecards, as has been discussed, the negative issues, particularly many of the most significant ones, can have, more often, negative effects. After all, far more people would rather have a real or, at the very least, personalized ecard. A list of negative items is shown below.

Positive ecards	Negative ecards
Timely reminders	April Fool's
Ecology	Hoaxes
Beneficial reminders	Insulting ecards
Educational ecards	Errors possible
Often free	Providing personal info
Convenient	Malware
Time saving	No longer unique unless signed digitally
Can be sent at the last moment	Can be interpreted as spam
Easy accessibility	Can be forwarded (bad if opinionated)
Can be animated in many ways	One should never send an ecard to a potential employer
Charities, humane causes, philanthropy	

One of the many changes email has manifested in communications has been a large shift in changing traditional notification for social events. Although ecards have had negative impacts on many aspects of email and Netiquette, there are also positive aspects, a number of which are listed above.

Chapter XV - Email Maintenance

"An ounce of prevention is worth a pound of cure."

- Benjamin Franklin

It may seem that email maintenance has little relationship to email Netiquette. This is far from true. Individuals, companies, and groups share common obligations to ensure optimal conditions exist for operation timeliness as well as for reliable sending and receiving of messages.

Performance

Many factors contribute to email performance, although some items might be beyond one's control (e.g., business networks, service providers, or defective components). However, many other conditions can be maintained and kept in good working order by even the most basic user.

Basic email distribution

Among the items that even the single user can and should control are proper mailbox size, regular checking of junk-mail lists, consistent mail backup, and regular archiving of all email folders. If a user uses a phone for email, this device should be regularly synchronized with other desktops and laptops to avoid having multiple mail threads in different locations. Moreover, synchronization ensures that appropriate backup will be in place in case of a system's losing large amounts of data. Most companies, service providers, and software products have services or utilities to assist in these functionalities.

The process of mailbox maintenance

Individual users should make determinations of the proper management they need to optimize the best use of time, resources, and Netiquette behavior. Replying intervals have been discussed in previous chapters. At times, immediate replies aren't possible because more information is needed. In order to ensure that responses to messages are done in a timely manner and without inordinate time and energy devoted to managing email, a maintenance process should be implemented.

Separating business and personal process

Business email Netiquette should be set up to make sure that business messages are received, read, replied to, stored, and managed properly. The last enables easy access and review. This is of great value when older correspondences need to be collected and sent along as soft copy. There are many compelling situations that necessitate this.

It can prove to be embarrassing or costly not to keep ostensibly important messages at hand. Therefore, in developing an email policy process, the proper tools and understanding of their use need to be secured to allow these functions. This might be using flags indicating the need to follow up or to categorize for simple storage. Many products offer most of the applications to achieve this, and they will generally be available in most companies. If the businesses do not readily have these processes in place, it may be feasible to ask to have these implemented by appropriate staff or as individuals. If companies do not provide these tools or processes, they usually can be user defined. Specific ways to achieve this are folders or disks to store email by category, importance, etc.

Mailbox maintenance is a form of proactive Netiquette. Since one of the major breaches of Netiquette is to have messages not responded to, here are some basic mailbox maintenance suggestions to reduce the risks of email loss, temporarily or permanently.

1. Check all email at least twice a day.

2. Do not leave any message unread for a defined period of time.

3. Mark or file critical messages that cannot be immediately replied to. If it is urgent mail, place it in a calendar.

4. Be thorough in reading messages and their threads.

5. Deal with business email first, unless there are compelling reasons not to.

6. If a full answer will take longer than usual to reply to because of a need to get more information, send a note to explain this.

7. Maintain discipline and predictability in company or personal maintenance processes.

8. Check junk mail regularly for mistakenly filtered mail. Notify the sender that some emails may have been lost. One may want to ask the sender if there are outstanding messages that have not been replied to.

9. Keep all email lists up to date; delete old addresses.

10. Keep dictionaries up to date, and allow proper names to be entered.

11. Empty deleted and junk files regularly.

12. Back up on a regular basis.

13. Remove all references such as "Sent from my... (Smartphone brand name)."

14. Provide off-hour schedules.

15. Notify all users forty-eight hours ahead of time when performing tasks that will slow down or shut down email services.

16. Keep security policies.

Policies for removing spam, junk mail, and chain mail

There is a certain amount of unwanted email that a person will receive, regardless of firewalls, filters, and anti-spam products. The vast majority of these will be from unknown sources. Some will be repetitive solutions from known organizations to which, as users, people have in some way provided their contact information. There will also be some chain or group emails, sent from known individuals, that might offer anecdotes, off humor, or some form of political or satirical expression.

When any of these messages are delivered, there should be a policy to effectively delete, act upon, or move them. This should be done in a timely manner as part of a maintenance routine—most particularly in business accounts. If these remain in a person's inbox, it might be assumed from an authorized person examining them that the person who holds them has a reason. Take, for example, an unsolicited job description. Perhaps a message is delivered from a competitive company. Or there may be services or products that are X-rated. Similarly, messages from friends with political or ethnic overtones or off-color humor may have been sent in jest, as satire, or as inside humor.

In order to most effectively deal with overflowing mailboxes with large percentages of "bad mail," processes should be employed to cut down on these emails. When job solicitations arrive, the recruiter should be notified—off hours and via personal email—not to send such communiqués to the business account. Obviously, offline communications can still occur if desired. When solicitations of dubious content are removed, they should be flagged as junk mail and immediately deleted permanently. Once again, these should not be opened or responded to, even by selecting "Remove." Similarly, most email users receive broadcast off-color messages, sometimes from acquaintances. If the sender is known, this person should be notified—again, offline—and told not to send these. When the users are unknown, the same actions apply to explicit emails.

Chapter XVI - Advanced Netiquette

> **"This report, by its very length, defends itself against the risk of being read."**
>
> - Winston Churchill

Wordiness

During the course of a busy day, receiving a long and detailed email is seldom welcomed. Worse still, the longer a correspondence is, the less likely it is to be read. There also is a distinct possibility that even if it is read, it may not be read completely or with full attention.

If a long email is necessary, the proper Netiquette should be followed to ensure readability: for example, the early introduction of a major topic and a brief explanation for the need to have a long message. It may also be best to have the correspondence divided and sent separately.

One long-term negative factor of sending a long or verbose message is that it may set a bad precedent in which the recipient will not immediately or ever read future correspondence.

Simple steps to avoid wordiness

Certain phrases can contribute to make sentences less clear as well as providing more verbosity. Among these are the following:

- Kind of

- Sort of

- For all intents and purposes

- Due to the fact

- Basically, actually

- As previously stated

- Generally speaking

- In particular

- Generally, in general

Redundant words and appositives

An appositive is defined (by reference.com) as a word or phrase to identify, amplify, or rename the preceding word. These can be unnecessarily obvious. Samples of appositives that add no value are shown below:

Wordy:	This is an example of an appositive that provides unnecessary identification. George Washington, the first president of the United States and a founding father…
Better:	George Washington, the first president…
Best	George Washington…

Redundant pairs

Most email writers cannot avoid using redundant pairs, and this is a common mistake made even in brief messages. Some generic examples of these follow:

- past   remembrances

- basic   fundamentals

- true   facts
- honest   truth
- terrible   tragedy
- final   outcome
- unexpected   surprise
- past   history
- future   plans
- boundary   line

There are many, many more of these, and the best way to reduce their usage is to edit text before sending.

Redundant categories

Email senders can reduce verbosity by being mindful to avoid descriptions that are not necessary:

large in size

oftentimes

of a bright color

heavy in weight

period in time

round in shape

at an early time

economic field

of cheap quality

in a confused state

Run-on sentences

These are the opposite of sentence fragments. The basic attribute of the run-on sentence is that there are two or more complete, independent clauses that lack a separating comma, semicolon, or conjunction. This wordiness can cause confusion or the necessity to reread the information. Usually, this can be corrected by a simple insertion of correct punctuation marks or conjunctions.

> **"Precision of communication is important, more important than ever in our era of hair-trigger balances when a false or misunderstood word may create as much disaster as a sudden thoughtless act."**
>
> - James Thurber

Some emails may be completely composed of a run-on sentence or sentences and can be most confusing, as shown in the following example:

Incorrect: The email will reach you soon kindly call after five minutes we can speak then.

Correct: The email will reach you soon; kindly call after five minutes, and we can speak then.

Incorrect: My email dated September 15 not only long and complex, but error ridden, perhaps not detailed but harsh in tone, cannot excuse the damage done to you perhaps but with this follow-up note we can have a fresh start as we do realize that compensation may be necessary.

The above run-on sentence comprises three independent sentences. These constitute an entire email and remove any reasonable, positive tone because of the confusion they create. It can be corrected as follows.

Correct: My email dated September 15 is not only long and complex and lacking detail but also error-ridden and harsh in tone; I cannot excuse the damage done to you. Perhaps with this follow-up note we can have a fresh start. We do realize that compensation may be necessary.

The punctuation provided in the above paragraph provides far more clarity and a better positive tone. Netiquette always assumes good grammar, punctuation, and lucidity.

Sentence fragments

Immediately behind email short-hand, the second leading Netiquette grammatical mistake is the area of sentence fragments. Typically, sentence fragments resemble real sentences; some can be quite long. They begin with a capital letter, conclude with an end mark, and lack an independent main clause. One should be mindful of common mistakes that contribute to or cause incomplete sentences.

> **"Complete sentences convey complete thought."**
>
> - Anonymous

Dependent clauses begin with subordinating words:

Subordinate Clause	A number of words missing either a noun or a verb
Present participle	Verb + ing
Infinitive	To + verb
Afterthought Fragment	Especially, for example, for instance, like, such as, including, except, because
Verb Fragment	No noun (i.e., Am at home)
Intentional Fragment	Not a chance, great to hear

Intentional fragments are acceptable from a Netiquette definition but should only be used informally. Without a full, completed sentence, there are a number of undesired message outcomes. Misinterpreted tone is one of these, misunderstood content is another, and the chance of a disrespectful reaction is still another. Again, it should be kept in mind that brevity does not necessarily relate to efficiency. This is particularly true for the recipient, as a fragment may require rereading a message or awaiting more words of clarification.

Words that most often begin a sentence fragment:

after	since	whereas
although	so	wherever
as	so that	whether
because	than	which
before	that	whichever
even if	though	while
even though	unless	who
if	until	whoever
in order	when	whom
that	whenever	whomever
once	where	whose
provided that		And many "ing" words

Common email fragments

1. See you
2. Talk to you later
3. Be there soon
4. What on earth
5. No problem
6. Twelve days to go
7. Hope all is well
8. Maybe later
9. Looks like rain
10. No way

Misplaced modifier

This is a common element in hastily written messages. A definition of a misplaced modifier is a word or clause not properly connected with the word it modifies.

Wrong:	The email that you sent me has a bad writer's Netiquette.
Corrected:	The email that you sent me has a writer's bad Netiquette.

The sentence can easily be corrected by moving the modifier. This is an easily identifiable mistake and would be seen if edited prior to sending a message. Both adjective and adverbs can be misplaced modifiers. Some of the most common adverbs intrinsically cause more common misplacement. These include *often, only, just, nearly*, and *merely*.

Wrong:	I wrote him only three emails.
Corrected:	Only I wrote him three emails.

The first sentence reads that one sent three messages. The second sentence reads that the writer was the only person to send the recipient three emails.

Indirect question

Indirect questions wrongly punctuated are a common misuse of grammar. Once again, a small amount of attention or detail can easily prevent this type of mistake. Most often, an indirect question is the result of an unnecessary question mark: "I wanted to ask you about leaving tomorrow?"

Usually this error can be corrected by removing the question mark: "I wanted to ask you about leaving tomorrow."

Another example is, "When the email reaches you after five minutes can you call?" This is easily corrected by, "When the email reaches you, can you call after five minutes?"

The subtle request or answer

There are many instances where individuals are not comfortable with providing straightforward intentions when sending emails. These include the areas of bad news, requesting favors, or refusals, all of which precipitate a "camouflage" of the main item to be presented. Although this methodology might be productive in face-to-face or verbal communications, it can be counterproductive with email. The following example is a good representation of not wanting to create any negatively to a situation that appears to be against the email receiver.

From:	Ike Bower
To:	Mark Stanz
Subject:	Your Promotion

Hello Mark:

How was your weekend? Were you able to take the NetiquetteIQ test? We are planning on doing this on Friday. I have received your emails RE your promotion. Will you check back with us later this quarter? None of our directors seem to have agreed to it. Maybe after the holidays there will be a change.

Give my best to all.

Thank you,

Ike Bower,

Director

ABC, Inc.

Delivery of bad news

It has been stated in other chapters of this book that the primary fact or purpose of an email should be included in the subject field and addressed quickly, before much less important content. There are both obvious and less obvious reasons for doing so. First, some emails are delayed in being read, dropped after a quick scan of the content, or not read at all. The classic example of emails like these is the one that, after a long message, ends with "P.S. Your pet has died."

Mixed message

Another method where the primary goal is sometimes buried within a message is the use of one or more sentiments or statements to soften what is often a request for a favor or gratuity. The example below is an exaggeration of such a message:

From: Paul
To: james@anyoldaddress.biz
Subject: How are you?

Hello Jim,

I just wanted to see how you have been. We are all well here and will be going on vacation soon. Was your holiday eventful? We need to get together soon.

By the way, I wanted to ask you if you will do me a favor and let us use your time-share next week? I will give you a call tomorrow and give you the dates.

Clearly this is "message mixing," where the sender perhaps had only one intention in mind. The impact of the tone manipulation might actually produce a more negative effect than anticipated and contribute to having the request rejected. If the introductory sentiments are indeed genuine, they are better off expressed in a separate email. By doing this, the sender can avoid not only the repercussions that might follow but also possibly the unease that the mixed messages may evoke.

> "When a book, any sort of book, reaches a certain intensity of artistic performance, it becomes literature. The intensity may be a matter of style, situation, character, emotional tone, or idea, or half a dozen other things."
>
> - Raymond Chandler

What is tone in an email?

Tone is the experience in a message that conveys or affects the respective author's attitude toward the topic or recipient. In writing email, how something is said and received is as critical as what is said. Physical interaction allows for body language, direct contact, and all the personal factors that contribute to effective communication. More subtle actions, such as humor, mild sarcasm, lighthearted comments, and unusual vocabulary contribute to possible misunderstanding. For those recipients with whom communication has occurred, consistency and variation both contribute significantly to the subjective reception of an email reader.

Proper Netiquette can have a greater effect upon how a user opens, reads, and reacts to a message. This is explained in chapter II: how a subject-line description, salutation, overall layout, and signature can set a tone before any content is read. If a subject line contains text such as "YOU MUST READ!!!" the recipient might interpret this as anger or sensationalism. To repeat what was stated in chapter II: lack of capitalization might be regarded as an insult to the reader. Similarly, the lack of a title in a salutation may also represent an insult. Caution should also be taken with stating or implying what someone "must" do, unless the sender has authority to do so.

Tone is reflected in an appropriate salutation based upon specific relationships and situations. Omission of a salutation often starts the email off in a tone that is rarely positive. Example A omits a proper salutation; example B includes one:

A. We cannot attend your dinner.

   Regards,

   The Smiths

B. Dear Sam:

   We cannot attend your dinner.

Regards,

The Smiths

Similarly, the omission of a closing can affect the tone of an entire message.

A. Dear Sam:

We cannot attend your dinner.

The Smiths

B. Dear Sam:

We cannot attend your dinner.

Regards,

The Smiths

In example A, with a single-word omission--regards--the tone might be interpreted as dismissive, disrespectful, or disinterested, especially since an explanation was not provided.

A recipient can also perceive a negative tone when a sender changes specific attributes by dropping or changing a single sentence, word, or structure element.

A. Dear Sam:

We will not be able to attend your dinner this weekend.

Thank you,

Ben

B. Dear Sam:

As much as we wish to see all of you, we will not be able to attend your dinner this weekend.

Respectfully,

Ben

The first example here does not include any personalization. If this is intentional, clearly the sender is demonstrating a negative tone. This will, perhaps, result in an experience by the recipient that differs from what has normally been felt in previous communications. What has been evidenced so far in this segment is that even a single word can change the tone and perception of an email. So can a change of "typical" expected formats and routines. The differences in tone and perceived emotion can become more dramatically different with each change in vocabulary, structure, or sender tone.

Tone—please and thank-you are the golden pair

Just as in etiquette, no matter what the circumstances, country, or time in history, Netiquette sits on a foundation of a few key words. We are all schooled from an early age to use *please* and *thank-you*. However, one must take care to use these words and many other "polite" words correctly, within proper tone and contrast. For example, consider the sentence "Call me ASAP." This sentence is in the imperative mode, meaning it is essentially a command (or appears to be). Next consider by contrast the sentence, "Will you please call me tomorrow or as soon as is convenient?" This certainly does not carry an imperative sense of command. Using a structure or tone similar to the first example would also be potentially damaging if addressed to a superior or someone with whom one is not familiar.

Next, consider the sentence, "Thank you for finally replying." This can easily be interpreted as sarcasm, even when the real context is that one's email has been inoperative. Next, compare this to the sentence, "Finally, I am able to thank you for your reply." Clearly, this has a better tone and would be interpreted positively more often. So even with the golden-pair words, Netiquette requires more than usage of them to be effective.

Additionally, one should be careful not to use gratitude in advance: "Your resolution of this problem will be appreciated" or "Thank you in advance for signing our petitions." Both of these sentences likely will appear presumptuous or obnoxious. Issuing a preemptive thank-you to further one's agenda is clearly not in the spirit of Netiquette. Many will see through this transparent behavior, to the detriment of the sender.

Most other Netiquette words, such as kindly or grateful, among others, do not pose quite the same potential for misuse, but any word can be stated with the wrong intent, tone, or with sarcasm. In summary, it is just as important to maintain sincerity in addition to polite language in order for your Netiquette to be effective and successful.

Tone and emotion

There are more than fifty identifiable positive emotions and more than fifty negative emotions. The tone conveyed by a sender's email can be perceived as any number of these in any combination. Messages can be interpreted by the sender, recipient, or third-party reader as vastly different. Even a single email can evoke feelings on extreme ends of the emotional spectrum. Messages sent to groups can also trigger extremely divergent emotions with each individual. With all of these potential misunderstandings, the following actions can tremendously reduce misunderstandings, unintended effects, and potential long-term damages or regrets.

1. Consistency—maintain Netiquette discipline—this is a big step

2. Mental intent—a sender should decide what the real purpose of an email should be before sending it

3. Patience

4. Review

5. Recite out loud

6. Imagine oneself as the recipient

7. Consider any ambivalence

8. Keep the ego out of email

9. Maintain discussion to the salient issues

10. Do not make presumptions about how comments will be perceived

Mirroring

One very subtle element of tone, in a positive sense, is mirroring, or imitation of style. First coined by Charles Caleb Cotton in 1821, the above adage is one of the most frequently heard, and with good reason. When corresponding with someone partly or totally unknown, imitation

> **"Imitation is the sincerest form of flattery."**
>
> - Charles Caleb Cotton

can prove to be a very nice way to establish a rapport with the correspondent. To achieve this, it is necessary to pay close attention to the tone and humor the recipient has maintained. Examine the parts of the email, starting with the subject line. Did the sender provide a detailed salutation? Is the style formal or on a first-name basis? Be alert if this changes, as it sometimes will.

Body of text—Is there usually a polite sentence or two, or does the correspondent avoid any informality and get directly to the issue at hand? Are sentences and paragraphs brief or lengthy? Is the vocabulary simple or polysyllabic? Does the tone imply more politeness or more of a commandeering attitude? Is punctuation and attention to detail evident?

Signature—Look for formality or familiarity in the signature, in particular, a full name (first and last) or shortened first name (e.g., Bob, Jack). It is most important to be mindful of a nickname.

Signature detail—Some senders have no detail on any signature block. This item does not need to be changed for mirroring or style equivalency purposes.

Mottos, slogans, or inspirational footnotes should be avoided. However, if a correspondent uses them and shares a mutual affinity, this can be a very nice way to legitimately connect.

If, over a longer term, it happens that a less formalized tone evolves from the correspondent, it is a good time to match this. However, caution should be taken not to do so on a greater scale.

Chapter XVII - More Advanced Netiquette

> "Take advantage of every opportunity to practice your communication skills so that when important occasions arise, you will have the gift, the style, the sharpness, the clarity, and the emotions to affect other people."
>
> - Jim Rohn

Much of the earlier parts of this book have been focused upon the basics of Netiquette. These offer a foundation for understanding how simple habits, processes, and adherence to rules will have immediate effects for email senders and recipients alike. This chapter offers more powerful Netiquette concepts that can be extremely important not only in simple email but also with advanced formal communication.

Many of the concepts presented in this chapter will seem like grade school grammar deja vu. For others, some of the topics might be ones they would never have considered as part of Netiquette. Notwithstanding, having a rudimentary understanding of these will unquestionably build on Netiquette strength.

Imperative mood

Imperative mood is defined as a grammatical mood that expresses direct commands or requests. It is also used to signal a prohibition, permission, or any other kind of exhortation.

Using imperative mood, particularly in email, is one of the most easily misinterpreted modes of electronic communication. As has been stated earlier, when face to face, a large percentage of communication is in body language and audible tone or inflection. Imperative statements can be much more easily and accurately interpreted. These actions obviously do not exist with email.

When imperative mood or sentences are used in messages, the reactions are typically quite immediate. These effects will often be the dominant and lasting emotion, no matter what content follows. Unless one is in authority to issue commands or knows the recipient very well, direct imperative sentences should not be used without thought. Some of these (or their close variants) include the following:

A. Call me tomorrow (or even more strongly, call me at 7:00 am tomorrow).

B. Let's have a meeting tomorrow.

C. You should call me now.

Differences between a command and a suggestion

It can be very difficult to differentiate a command from a suggestion or appeal. Take the following example: "Let's meet in the office early tomorrow."

Is the above a command, request, or suggestion? By itself, it would be very difficult to tell. When a specific end result is desired, the sentence needs to be structured or expanded to clearly represent the sender's tone. If the above sentence is going to a subordinate, the message should be clear—it is a command.

Should the above message be addressed to a friend or close peer then we can be fairly certain that the sentence is an open invitation. Finally, when the same message is sent to a customer or less-than-familiar person, the message can, once again, be interpreted in several ways. The worst of these would be for the recipient to presume this was a command or an attempt to manipulate for a desired outcome. Proper email Netiquette espouses using suggestive words or phrases when a sentence can be read as a command. In this sentence, a far less imperative assumption can read: "I suggest we meet in the office tomorrow morning at 10:00 a.m. Is this a good time for you?"

Similarly, but in a more polite manner, the sentence can be stated: "Please meet me tomorrow in the office at 10:00 a.m. Is this convenient?"

Even better: "Please meet me tomorrow morning in the office, if this is convenient. Anytime close to 10:00 a.m. is best for me."

The following are imperative words or phrases that should be avoided or used carefully:

Let's…	Don't…
Call me…	You must…
You can't…	Be here at…
Stop…	You better…
Hold off…	Listen…

International email

As mentioned in chapter I, billions of email users are generating a volume of more than 500 billion messages per day in 2013. Clearly a significant percentage of these are international. Netiquette considerations within a country are expanded when communicating globally. These considerations include the following:

1. Time zones

2. Terms of address

3. Holidays and holy days

4. Acronyms, idioms, colloquialisms, and special names (slang)

5. Translations

6. Culture

7. Politics, humor sensitivities

8. Censoring

9. Formats of date and time

10. Attention to detail

11. Tone

12. Global traffic

13. Money

It has been shown in previous chapters that many particulars in communication are far harder or nearly impossible to convey via email. With foreign emails, these subtleties and differences are more numerous. What may be standard knowledge or normal behavior in one country is unacceptable, confusing, or even insulting in others.

Time zones

Although most recipients understand that differences in time dictate when a message will be received, delays will typically be more numerous and pronounced. If immediate answers are required, the sender and recipient should accommodate time-zone differences.

For example, the time difference between London and New York is five hours. If a sender in New York wishes to send a message and receive a same-day reply, this action should be taken early in the morning.

The closer to early afternoon an email is sent, the less likely a full-cycle email transaction can take place.

Therefore, if the New York emailer sends a message at 1:00 p.m. EST, on a Friday, it is reasonable to assume he will not read the reply until Monday afternoon (or Tuesday afternoon, if the Monday is a holiday). If an email, such as a videoconference invitation, is sent to several different international invitees, it should be done so with probably two days' notice in order to allow for ample time for everyone to reply.

One should also be mindful of religious and national holidays in the country where the message is being sent. Additionally, one should make the recipient aware if a holiday is going to fall in the sender's country when time issues are important. There are numerous lists of international holidays available. Microsoft Outlook provides one, and two Internet sources are www.cftech.com and when-is.com.

Acronyms can be doubly confusing to out-of-country contacts. When using any acronyms with an overseas recipient, it is critical to identify what the acronym stands for, particularly if it involves a technical entity or domestic organization.

Idioms and colloquialisms

Idioms can be as confusing to non-natives as acronyms are. Although it will be obvious to one from another country that they do not know an acronym's meaning, the reader may take the meaning of an idiom literally; he or she very well may spend considerably more time trying to discern the meaning of the idiom. Moreover, the reader may assume a wrong meaning to the idiom.

Colloquialisms and slang also are confusing to foreigners, even those within the same country. This is because colloquialisms and slang often originate in a particular geographic area or within a specific demographic (e.g., the South in the United States, or a province such as Hong Kong in China). Regardless, if international emails contain idioms, colloquialisms, slang, or acronyms, it is usually poor Netiquette to use these and a habit one should not fall into. Even when these are understood, they very well may come across as clichés or unprofessional.

Once again, here is a brief definition (from Merriam-Webster) of the terms discussed:

Term	Definition
Acronym	An abbreviation formed from a set of word's initial letters
Idiom	An expression, language, or dialect of a particular person, region, or class
Colloquialism	A local or regional dialect expression

Translation software

Great technical progress has been made in the area of translation software. While this capability can be useful in a simplified, casual venue, it is highly recommended that it be eschewed for business, or for complex or sensitive email, because there is no effective way to check grammar, tone, punctuation, or even accuracy. This type of tool can lead to a number of negative results. Many items cannot be translated easily, if at all––particularly tone.

Culture

Cultural considerations for Netiquette in international email closely resemble those for other forms of interaction and communication. Dates, monetary, and typographical conventions should be used and shown in the formats of all countries represented in the emails. The following is an example of these in a communication from the United States to the United Kingdom:

Dear Anthony, [salutation for a friend]

It was a pleasure speaking with you again. As we discussed, the cost of the widget you requested is £100. I have scheduled a call to discuss this situation for Tuesday, 20/1/2015, at 3 p.m. GMT (10 am EST).

Yours,

Alex Pushkin [Closing for a friendly acquaintance]

Politics

Every country in the world has specific political foundations. These obviously range from liberal to authoritarian. Just as Netiquette espouses neutrality in communicating any political judgments or opinions within a country, this code applies more strongly when communicating internationally. Even subtle comments can be misinterpreted or, worse still, lead to severe consequences to participants in certain countries. It is important to understand that just as emails exist "forever," any country has the means to intercept email and to prosecute even the most innocent political satire.

Elaborating upon one's own political preferences has no Netiquette value and can easily be misinterpreted. Once again, the premise is that no assumptions about a recipient's preferences should ever be made through email. Moreover, one should be mindful that emails can be forwarded, archived forever, or posted publicly. Because politics exist locally, regionally, and nationally, their effects can evoke prejudice or favoritism toward anyone engaging in them. Simply put, they do not mix well in all but the friendliest of audiences.

Censoring

There are countries that block email based on any number of parameters. Most of these parameters have been mentioned previously. One should be mindful of these possibilities when communicating internationally. There are a surprising number of countries where some form of censorship exists. Several internet reports (including Aliki Karasaridis, "Online censorship in 2012") have been published reviewing the number of countries filtering online content.

Formats for dates, times, money, and temperature

When representing various measurements in international mail, it should never be assumed the formats used by the originator will be understood by the recipient. This is particularly true with the United States. In this country, the standards of linear volume and temperature differ from the majority of other countries. Clearly, items related to weather, distance, temperature, weights, or costs should be accounted for.

Traffic

Global speed and deliverability vary dramatically throughout the world. According to Internet World Stats, the top twenty ranking countries in terms of Internet usage account for almost 76 percent of total world traffic. Most of these countries have competitive traffic and access costs. The remaining countries have far different situations and little, if any, choice in services or costs. Speeds, deliverability, and the company's reliability can be dramatically different.

These considerations should be noted by a sender when considering and awaiting replies. It should also never be assumed that deliverability is as reliable either. Because of these dynamics, attachments and their size should also be carefully considered.

> "Men are apt to mistake the strength of their argument. The heated mind resents the chill touch and relentless scrutiny of logic."
> - William E. Gladstone

Fallacies in logic and arguments

It has been stated earlier in these pages that good Netiquette is most often characterized with less verbose and more effective word usage. Nevertheless, even the simplest statements, paragraphs, or sentences can and should have not only good basics but also good logic, reasoning, and arguments. Even with perfect grammar, tone, content, and structure, poor logic or fallacies can significantly undermine the intent and content of even the simplest of emails.

The study of logic dates back to ancient Greece and has always been an integral part of reasoning and providing arguments or theories. There are some basic rules of logic that should always be applied to communication. The following identify some of these and provide some brief examples of how each can be misused:

1. False dilemma—This argument states that a solution must be one of two choices: *Either we support the war, or we are unpatriotic.*

2. *Ad hominem*—Using a personal part or belief of a person to prove an argument: *Because English is not his first language, he cannot write good emails.*

3. Straw man (*argumentum ad logicum*)—This statement generalizes a viewpoint and then belittles it by extending it beyond its original premise: *The president vetoed the oil companies' exemptions; therefore, he is against large corporations.*

4. Red herring (*ad misericordiam*)—This attempts to evoke pity to aid in a request: *This job should be given to me because I have not worked in two years.*

5. Slippery slope (*non sequitur*)—This fallacy assumes one action or condition will lead to a different condition: *If I am not hired for this position, your customers will buy from someone else.*

6. Repetitive argument (*argumentum ad nauseam*)—This is an assertion made over and over to try to prove a point: *As I have told you in my last three emails, you should give my staff a raise to increase productivity.*

7. *Argumentum ad antiquitatum*—A statement that asserts something must be right because it has traditionally been done the same way: *We have never had email complaints, so there's no need to add disclaimers.*

8. *Argumentum ad numerum*—This is a deduction that, since a majority of people believe something, it is true: *Eighty percent of our employees do not believe we have to answer customer emails within twenty-four hours, so our corporate policy should be to reply within one week.*

9. *Argumentum ad ignorantiam*—This fallacy specifically assumes something is correct because it has not been proven otherwise: *My emails are well written, because no one has ever complained about them.*

10. *Tu quo que*—This is the "you too" argument that counters a mistake or fallacy by claiming the accuser has done the same: *You claim my emails are rude in content, but so are yours.* Although the statement may be true, it does not make the mistake correct simply by stating that someone else does it.

11. Begging the question (*petitio principii*)—This logic abuse uses the same statement in a premise as in its conclusion: *Our company's employee emails are great because we studied the best email tutorials and we write great emails.*

12. Moral equivalence—This argumentative fallacy begins with a statement and concludes with a moral exaggeration: *We will win because our side is more caring.*

13. Hasty generalization—This is a theory or conclusion made with a paucity of collaborative information. *This has been a very cool summer, so there is no such thing as global climate change.*

14. *Cum hoc, ergo propter hoc* (with this, therefore because of this)—This asserts that because two loosely related items occur simultaneously, each has a direct causal effect on the other: *During the last five years, whenever our team has had a lead in the last quarter, we have won. We are now leading starting the last quarter, so we will win.*

15. Fallacy of a complex question—These are forms of wrong dilemmas that only offer one solution: *Is it true you've stopped spanking your children?*

Hazardous emails

Recently, the American Management Association (AMA) and ePolicy Institute conducted a survey and found 80 percent of 526 companies had a formal email policy. There are no longer excuses for errors in emails (from a legal, corporate, or personal perspective). Appropriate Netiquette extends beyond the commonsense basic values contained in its core principals. Netiquette encompasses the privileges that individuals are afforded and entrusted with during employment.

Much like using a desk, kitchenette, or audiovisual equipment at one's place of employment, the email infrastructure is the property of the employer and is owed respect, consideration, and requisite adherence to both common sense and implicit corporate rules. Netiquette encompasses respect and adherence for the following:

1. Maintaining the company's reputation

2. Preventing sexual or illegal workplace harassment

3. Defamation, libel

4. Data leakage

5. Compliance violation (HIPPA, etc.)

Topics to avoid

1. Terrorism

2. Committing crimes

3. Sexual explicitness

4. Conspiratorial dialogue

     A. Delete this

     B. No one will find out

     C. Is this legal?

     D. What happens if we get caught?

     E. Or else!

     F. Unless this is done, then…

5. Racism

6. Sexism

7. Violence

8. Sedition

9. Extreme hatred or anger

10. Revenge

11. Toxic emails (this is a figurative term for damaging)

12. Employment change on business accounts

Emails about anyone's medical condition (e.g., chemotherapy, CT scan, MRI) should not be written. HIPPA legislation was enacted to ensure that people are protected against having their information exposed electronically.

One should always avoid using one's company name in a personal blog, as there may be a policy against it.

One should refrain from disclosing details such as financials, pricing, or technical details about another company outside the organization when a nondisclosure agreement may be in place.

Social invitations, such as a request for a date, are to be avoided on company email. If sexual harassment is ever claimed, there is an electronic record. This can be, arguably, a form of proof.

Chapter XVIII - Netiquette for Children and Young Adults

> **"Our technological powers increase, but the side effects and potential hazards also escalate."**
>
> - Alvin Toffler

Epolicy for children

One of the most sensitive segments of epolicy and Netiquette is the area of children's usage of email and the Internet. These are some of the major categories to consider:

1. Rules

2. Bullying

3. Safety

4. Courtesy

5. Education

6. Emergency aid and assistance

Application of Netiquette, good habits, and correct grammar are essential routines throughout life. Negative patterns can easily end up being used in school and social life into adulthood. No one will dispute the absolute need to have protection for children using email and the

Internet. The same principles apply to texting, social groups, and other popular online activities. However, there are other considerations that have both short-term and long-term ramifications.

Young people are now increasingly using electronic communication in lieu of face-to-face, written, or telephone contact. Arguably, children and young adults who have begun their methods of communication via email, Twitter, and texting have decreased knowledge of basic formal writing skills and Netiquette. Unfortunately, these habits and behavior translate into not only the items mentioned above but also may promote behavior that allows for and facilitates lack of respect, abundance of informality, and the inability to understand the measure one's words have on others.

Safety

The premiere consideration when children and young people access the Internet, email, texting, or Twitter is safety. In order to maximize this, it is critical to educate and provide a list and processes for young users. These rules offer a good comprehensive starting point for young people that considers their point of view:

1. Never use communicative technology when biking, driving, crossing busy streets, or in hazardous situations.

2. Always ask your parents' permission before using your full name, address, telephone number, or school name anywhere on the Internet.

3. Always tell your parents or guardians if you see something online that you know is wrong or that makes you feel uncomfortable.

4. Don't respond to messages that make you feel uncomfortable or uneasy.

5. Never give out a credit card number or password.

6. Never send out your picture without your parents' permission.

7. Be careful when someone offers you something, such as gifts or money, for nothing.

8. Don't ever accept a gift or an offer that involves having someone visit your house.

9. Never arrange to meet someone in person whom you've met online, unless you discuss it with your parents and an adult goes with you.

10. Talk to your parents to set up rules for going online. Decide with them the best time of day to be online, the length of time to be online, and appropriate areas to visit.

11. Get to know your "online friends" just as you get to know all of your other friends. Be sure that you are dealing with someone whom you and your parents know and trust before giving out any personal information about yourself via email.

12. Be respectful.

13. Avoid electronic bullying.

14. Do not open attachments from senders you do not know.

15. Do not deploy spyware or any other malicious or compromising programs or software.

16. Do not use other people's email accounts.

17. Report email abuses.

18. Educate your friends when you see they do not follow these guidelines.

19. Minimize webspeak (i.e., short words, emoticons, and slang).

20. Do not use foul language (i.e., no swearing).

21. Do not criticize people who might read your message later. Any mail can be forwarded or inadvertently sent.

22. Remember: whatever you write will be stored somewhere **forever**.

23. Avoid "flaming" or insulting someone.

24. Tell others to stop when they use foul language.

25. Log off immediately when done.

26. Do not be afraid to ask a trusted adult for guidance.

Courtesy

Children and young adults should be taught that all electronic communication should adhere to Netiquette and courtesies one would expect from interaction with others. The rules of public behavior and consideration do not vanish because of the lack of direct contact. As has been set forth elsewhere in this book, email is one of the least effective methods of communication and requires as much consideration as possible.

Education

Children and teenagers should become educated in all aspects of safety, courtesy, and Netiquette as they begin using the Internet. Time and care should be taken, on a regular basis, to verify the safety, ethical behavior, and courtesy items discussed throughout this book. Young users should be certified as to knowledge when new technologies and trends emerge. Parents should make themselves aware of these new developments and incorporate them into education policies for their children.

When policies and rules have been defined, these should be printed and posted near the computer work area. Similarly, a file or folder should be placed on all computer desktops.

Enforcement and discipline

It is up to each parent to maintain policies to assure that Netiquette and safety are maintained. Additionally, parents need to determine times of access and usage. If these rules and guidelines are not met, it should be made clear what the consequences are. It is recommended that all minors understand that their communications are subject to inspection. Whatever guidelines, rules, policies, or considerations are put into place, it is essential that these be clearly defined. Similarly, once these have been put into place, it is also very important that violations be dealt with consistently.

Monitoring and reporting

Many tools and services are available to assist parents in viewing children's usage and activities, even altering these tools in real time when children compromise parents' viewing policies. Almost any policy regarding capture, accessibility, storage, and filtering can be implemented at the parents' discretion and changed when required.

Parental responsibilities

Parents' roles in epolicy for their children should not stop at defining family viewing guidelines but should also include assuring full safety, physical security, Internet security, and prevention of personal data loss. These measures should be similar to those provided to adults. All devices that children have access to should have full virus and firewall protection. Passwords should be used for all portable devices or those that may be accessed by others. Consideration should also be given to prevent data leakage by external devices such as USB and DVD drives as well. This would apply to having encrypted or password-protected files on all removable media in case of loss. Laptop computers should have a GPS function, if possible.

Part of a parental epolicy routine should also include regular checks on email, website visits, and time spent on Internet activities. Updating filters and content options should also be part of this routine. Vigilance will never prove to be hurtful and can obviously prevent undesired events. If these actions are part of an ongoing process, they are far more likely to be well received by children and young adults who otherwise would object to any perceived constraints. Even though older children and young adults in particular may be against what may seem to them an invasion of privacy, it is far more crucial for parents to have control over potential or real perils. Indeed, as has been noted in chapter VII, when, as young adults or older, people will be employed by companies, their privacy rights in email or online activity will not exist.

Filtering and blocking inappropriate websites and groups is another key area of parental responsibility. There are many tools and services available to do these functions. Some software packages include multiple security products; many service providers have tools as well, and there are many products available in the marketplace. Since each passing day brings more risks, parents and supervisors of children and young adults should have services that will proactively find and block access to undesirable Internet sites and activities as well as provide strong virus, content, and malware software detection.

Email and messaging overuse

Children's email usage can, much like video games and television, become addictive and overwhelming. Many scientific studies have been and will continue to be conducted to measure trends and results of children's email usage. It falls to parents to be vigilant, not only to immediate safety dangers but also to long-term effects of email, messaging, and Internet use. Here are some behavior signs to look for:

1. Privacy demands

2. Crankiness

3. Changes in sleep habits

4. Suddenly lower grades

5. Fewer family and social interactions

6. Neglecting chores or normal responsibilities

7. Refusals to log off

8. Polite-language degradation

9. Changes in eating habits

10. Less outdoor and physical activity

Some electronic alternatives

Many parents or adults responsible for young people's use of technology will provide for periods or situations when or where technology use is not allowed. Some of these might include the following:

1. Meals

2. During homework

3. Attending formal events

4. "Quiet times"

5. After specific evening hours

6. Before defined morning hours

7. At school

8. In hazardous areas

9. At bedtime

10. When operating modes of transportation

Texting and email as emergency aids

Perhaps the most important element to justify children and teenagers' having advanced technology at their disposal is the protection technology can afford. Texting, GPS, email, Twitter, and even cameras can assist in helping those lost by providing directions, providing emergency notification, allowing tracing, or locating those missing. All children and teenagers should have every available item noted above implemented and, where possible, be trained on their uses. Doing this can conceivably save a young person's life.

Cyberbullying

One of the most egregious, appalling, and dangerous violations of Netiquette is cyberbullying. As many people are aware, it can produce humiliation, depression, rage, and even suicide.

Cyberbullying is defined as *a deliberate attempt through electronic media to do harm to an individual or group.*

Types of cyberbullying and their potential damage

There are various methods by which cyberbullying is unleashed. These include the following:

1. Harassment

2. Cyber stalking/spying

3. Impersonation

4. Threats—direct or indirect

5. Exclusion

6. Libel

7. Falsification

8. Misinformation

9. Mockery

10. Blackmail/extortion

Most of these items are self-explanatory, as they occur in non-technological form as well. School or other activities conclude at certain times, but electronic forms of communication operate 24/7. Events can also be programmed to occur. Any of these can contribute directly to humiliation, loss of revenue, diminished prestige, depression, isolation, or even suicide. Cyberbullying can also be worse than conventional bullying, in that it creates a permanent, traceable recorded item that can have a negative impact far into the future. Whatever transpires over the Internet or electronic communication, once disseminated, cannot be completely undone. Therefore, preventive and preemptive actions should be taken to reduce the potential effects of cyberbullying.

Cyberbullying guidelines for parents

Parents play by far the most critical role in preventing, recognizing, and eliminating cyberbullying. Just as good Netiquette begins as soon as young people are given access to electronic communication, cyberbullying rules and guidelines need to be implemented as soon as other aspects of Netiquette. Guidelines, rules, constant communication, vigilance, and swift action are all necessary to maintaining safe and productive cyber activity.

Preventive measures

The first steps for parents to take involve security measures for all devices. Most households have some types of protection, and these should be as comprehensive as possible. The following list outlines many of the essential ones:

1. Firewalls and traditional protection products such as spyware and identity protection

2. Service provider filters for websites and content

3. Rules for usage

4. Regular checkups and supervision

5. Regular discussions about usage: where, when, how

6. Familiarization with school programs for cyberbullying

7. Young people must be constantly encouraged to immediately report any bullying

8. An atmosphere of blamelessness should be established to encourage communication regarding bullying

9. Understanding of steps and measures to take when cyberbullying occurs is essential

10. Children and young adults need to constantly be assured and reassured that they have help available

Warning signs of cyberbullying: both sides

Although most of this chapter focuses on the victims of cyberbullying, there are also the bullies themselves to consider, and many of the same preemptive measures can be applied to prevent a child or young person from becoming one. All aspects of Netiquette should be introduced and practiced with regular communications. One should stay aware not only of school policies and programs but also if cyberbullying has been occurring. Specific warning signs of children or young adults participating in cyberbullying include the following:

1. Irritability when electronic media is not available

2. Negative changes in social behavior—particularly new friends

3. Dramatic cultural changes

4. Hiding of programs or screens

5. New or multiple email accounts

6. Usage of aliases

7. Animated behavior when using computers

8. Late-night usage

Once any proof of cyberbullying is realized, immediate steps must be taken. Professional assistance should be sought. Both age-appropriate and commonsense actions should be taken.

Warning signs of cyberbullying victimization

Some signs to be alert for when a child or young person is being victimized:

1. Sudden nervousness when receiving email or texting

2. Loss of enthusiasm for school or favorite social activities

3. Self-isolation or withdrawal

4. Changes in sense of humor

5. Alteration in appearance

6. Avoidance of computer projects and discussions

7. Changes in email account names

8. Noticeable mood downswings after using computers or electronic communication

Again, it should be stressed that constant communication, positive assurance of available help, and increased vigilance will, one hopes, provide for an environment of protection from the negative effects of cyberbullying. When normal and safe conditions for email and texting are in place for children and young adults, there are still issues, as discussed earlier in this chapter. No doubt, as technology moves forward, there will be more issues to contend with. Even if new technology holds no interest for a certain individual, one should, at the very least, keep up with and understand these changes. This will provide proactive benefits for keeping young users secure.

Texting

As S A now I mean 2 write
2 U sweet K T J,
The girl without a ‖
The belle of U T K.

I 1 der if U got that 1
I wrote 2 U B 4
I sailed in the R K D A,
And sent by LN Moore...

This S A, until U I C
I pray 2 U 2 Qs
And do not burn in F E G
My young & wayward muse.

Now fare U well, dear K T J,
I trust that U R true --
When this U C, then you can say,
An S A I O U."

—(with apologies to) Charles Carroll, 1860

> "Calling someone without texting first is the new showing up unannounced."
>
> - Unknown

With the emergence of more small devices with email capabilities, the quality of email composition and Netiquette has eroded even further and rapidly. Many of the applications that operate on these platforms do not have the full functionality and tools that a desktop or laptop product does. These might include spell-checking, vocabulary lookup, auto-completion, and more.

Generally, the same basics of Netiquette that apply to the composition of email discussed within this book should be applied to smaller devices. However, certain processes necessitate a greater or lesser emphasis. For example, if a spell-checker is not available, more care should be given to manual editing. Additionally, more time should be spent to ensure that capitalization, punctuation, and removal of unnecessary threads is provided more attention.

Because of space, time, and other constraints, some practices of Netiquette may require a reduction: for example, including the text of previous questions that one is replying to or reducing the number of message recipients.

Signatures should still be used. Include a Bcc or Cc to yourself in order to ensure messages have been delivered. Since the display screens for texting are smaller, it is critical to keep messages even shorter, clearer, and less cluttered than standard emails. As tempting as it may be, abbreviations should, as with emails, be kept at an absolute minimum.

Text messages are delivered to devices that are usually with the person to whom the text is sent. This can be good if a message needs to be delivered quickly or if the recipient is out of the office. It may be tempting, but multiple text messages should be avoided, as these may be a source of interruption or annoyance. Consideration should also be given to the following:

Texting dos and don'ts

Do	Don't
Think before you send	Convey bad or very sad news
Let someone know your phone number	Text at late hours–– people may still have phones on
Establish a reply policy	Text where doing so may be a distraction
Expect reasonable reply time	Participate in text games
Lock your keypad when not in use	

Chapter XIX - Inferences, Assumptions, and Presumptions

> ## "Dr. Livingstone, I presume."
> - H.M. Stanley, 1871

There is often confusion about the definitions for inferences, assumptions, and presumptions. When any of these are part of an email, each can create confusion enough to change the desired purpose of a communication. As stated previously in this book, any message written in haste can fail in its intent or even worsen a situation one is trying to correct.

Here are some basic definitions:

Inference—Something we take for granted often because of a related observation or experience or something that is factually known; that is, an educated guess.

Assumption is an accepted thing thought to be true but without proof—something taken for granted, an axiom or starting point in an argument or theory, a natural deduction. "You have to start somewhere."

Presumption—*Omnia praesumtur rite esse acta*: Latin proverb that means "all things are presumed to be done in due form." A presumption is taken to be the case, based upon reasonable evidence--an idea that has always been believed to be right, taken for granted, not likely to be wrong. Best possible guess or conclusion.

Over-assuming is usually a guess based on unverified information; when inferences, assumptions, or presumptions are made, obvious risks are involved. Because of the inherent possibilities that email, by its structure, can evoke, even more misunderstandings are likely to occur. Faulty assumptions can be trivial or significant, but many can be avoided with Netiquette principles and practices. As the tools and technologies available become more sophisticated, their impact creates more assumptions. A good example of this is the MS Outlook grammar check. Although helpful, it is far from infallible and can, at times, be off the mark quite considerably. This is evidenced by rationalizations that lower standards, which tolerate mistakes and due diligence, are all acceptable. The long-term trend of all of these factors—email structure, increasingly sophisticated technology, and lowering standards—increase the complacency about email senders being subpar in communication skills.

Perception—An experience from the senses or, at times, intuition. Not yet taken for granted.

Thoroughness, clarity, and objectivity will greatly eliminate the gray areas that inference, assumption, and presumption can create. All people make multiple inferences and assumptions every day, including what and how recipients of email will conclude and the degrees of the receivers' reactions in reading the correspondence. To be skillful in effective email writing, it is necessary to not only employ Netiquette but also to have a basic idea of those habits that can undermine one's accuracy and effectiveness in communication.

Examples of inference and assumption

The following list summarizes some common inferences and assumptions.

1. A correspondence has been read or opened.

2. Intended emotions have been understood.

3. Specific urgency has been properly addressed.

4. Privacy will be maintained.

5. Any requests or demands will be honored.

6. The recipient wishes to receive correspondence.

7. An intended goal is accomplished.

8. Recipients will have universal reactions.

9. Schedules for meetings, calls or participatory events are open.

10. Assumptions concerning a recipient's age, race, politics, marriage, or religion

11. The addressees will ask for clarification if emails are unclear to them.

12. If replies are not either immediate, short-cycled (i.e., responded to within a requested timeframe), or not replied to at all, the addressee is categorically rejecting the sender.

Complaints

Creating an effective complaint email can be particularly challenging in maintaining Netiquette. By the time a complaining email is composed and sent, there is probably a significant amount of time, loss of service, or inconvenience, and, most significantly, anger and frustration. The general inclination for many would be a communication with rough language, reprimands, threats, demands, and unmistakably negative tone.

Unlike face-to-face complaints, an email can be ignored, quickly discarded, never read, or be "auto replied" to. In order to increase the likelihood of a complaint having some results and effects, the following items should be taken into consideration:

1. Use all forms of Netiquette.

2. Identify the proper recipients.

3. Determine the processes companies have put into place, and follow them.

4. Be concise.

5. State what the expected result was presumed or intended to be.

6. State what the result actually was and provide the difference of relevant effects (i.e., loss of time, money, or other negative impact).

7. Detail a solution—be specific. Include reasonable goals, such as time to resolve, objectives, or needs.

8. Request a response with a realistic schedule.

9. Verify you have addressed the correct person or department. Ask for the right one if needed.

10. Request a response that your correspondence has been received. (This is not number eight above, which is a resolution outline.)

11. Show open-mindedness and willingness to cooperate rather than a demand for a single solution.

Following up an email complaint

Once the email has been sent, allow a reasonable response time, as determined previously. If no response is received, a resend should be sent with a "Second request" as part of the subject line:

To: Customerservice@abcwidget.com

From: Cyrus Pericles

Re: ABC Wiget product—Second request, Please read/reply ABC Widget

If there is no answer again, then a different approach should be taken, with an escalation, if possible. One option is to send the same email to the webmaster. Webmaster is a generic term used to identify and describe the person responsible for maintaining a website. Usually a website has an address to contact this person, i.e., webmaster@

netiquetteiq.com. Another is to attempt to ascertain additional names of those in responsible positions.

Complaint readers

It is worth keeping in mind that those who read and act upon complaints probably have dozens they read daily. Surely they have fielded almost every type of negative email category imaginable. Logically, it can be assumed that the more polite a particular correspondence is, the more likely a positive result will transpire.

Bad email complaint example:

To: Customerservice@abcwidget.com

From: Gus Yeller

Subject: A very mad customer

I am writing to you as a very mad and upset customer. The piece of junk you call an ABC Widget is the worst thing I've ever bought. How do you stay in business?

I am demanding a refund immediately, and I can only hope your department isn't as bad as the product you represent. The sales receipt has been destroyed but you should have the order on file.

Good email complaint example:

To: Customerservice@abcwidget.com

From: Cyrus Pericles

Subject: ABC Widget Product

Dear Sir/Madam:

Last month, having previously enjoyed one of your products, I purchased an ABC Widget. However, this unit has not performed well. I have attempted to make it work by using the manual suggestions, but with no success. Also, your technical assistance was very responsive but unable to resolve the issue.

Unless you can put forth another possible solution, please arrange for me to return the unit. I have attached a copy of the receipt and warranty card. If I am required to communicate with someone else, kindly advise. Also, a confirmation that this email has been received would be appreciated. You will find all of my contact information below. Your prompt attention to these matters is welcomed.

Have a nice day.

Sincerely,

Cyrus Pericles
123 Agora Way
Athens, NJ 00001
555-123-4567 Day
555-123-6789 Evening

Clearly, the second example will almost always produce better results. The time and energy spent on each is equivalent. It should be kept in mind that the person, or people, who will read the email is not directly responsible for the problem. They may, however, be the ones who can make the decision on the outstanding issue, so, unless the sender of the email complaint is a very influential person, valued customer, or someone extra special, he or she will be better served by utilizing Netiquette. Furthermore, even if this person is a VIP, it will only enhance his or her status.

Chapter XX - Appointments

> "If I have made an appointment with you, I owe you punctuality. I have no right to throw away your time, if I do my own."
>
> - Richard Cecil

Making appointments

Email can greatly facilitate scheduling appointments, social meetings, online services, and many, many more personal, professional, and organizational activities. Often, the time saved in the planning, dissemination of information, and confirmation of events is significant. However, Netiquette can clearly suffer in many ways, sometime resulting in lost time, misunderstandings, and people waiting on the telephone, in front of a terminal, or at some location waiting for an event that was already moved or canceled.

Amazingly, many people will not think twice about canceling an appointment at the last minute, perhaps with others en route to a place, sometimes without the option of turning back or not even having access to email. It is important to provide invitees as much notice as possible when there is a legitimate reason to postpone or cancel a meeting or event, especially if the invitee needs extended travel, expense, or time.

Anyone who does postpone or cancel a meeting is changing another's day, sometimes significantly. As such, all care should be given to ensure that an event has a high certainty of occurring. To ensure that people can also attend, as much as reasonable, provide as much lead time as possible. If an appointment is scheduled by regular conversation or telephone, an immediate confirmation should be sent via email. If most of the proposed attendees have access to calendaring, this works nicely in automating schedules, allowing for automated changes and cancellations, and for editing details such as location, agenda, conference call information, or online meeting particulars.

It all too often occurs that invitations are sent out that abandon any attempt to accommodate all or as many invitees as possible. This can result in the snowball message, where even just a few invitees begin a stream of "reply to all" mail that can transpire for days, ultimately not coming to a resolution until after the first scheduled date! This results in even more snowball messages and, at times, the abandonment of an event altogether.

Puzzlingly enough, many appointments and invitations are sent with only a single time and date offered, when it would be quite simple and save a great deal of traffic and overhead to propose several dates and times. When possible, follow the procedure of offering three different times on at least two separate days (e.g., Monday at 1:00 p.m. EST, Tuesday at 11:00 a.m. EST, or Tuesday at 3:00 p.m. EST). If multiple time zones are involved for conference calls or video presentations, state the specific zones of the invitees (i.e., 4:00 p.m. EST [1:00 p.m. PST]). Anyone who has entered a conference call only to be the only one left or who is far too early because of a time-zone misunderstanding readily understands the Netiquette of including time zones.

The eternal email meeting

Email and the lack of Netiquette have spawned a new category of appointment: "TEEM" (the eternal email meeting). Since email allows indefinite last-minute changes and postponements, many people postpone meetings time after time, often for weeks or months. As can be expected, a significant amount of these end up not occurring at all. This can be frustrating to all the attendees. Good Netiquette might have prevented a host of these TEEMS, and consequent loss of time, strain on relationships, damaged reputations, and frustration and resentment. It is in keeping with proper Netiquette that, when an appointment, meeting, or event is committed to in writing, a best effort be made to accommodate everyone.

Some individuals do not know how--or find it difficult--to say no to a request to meet. Others may have ambivalence about meeting and resort to postponing an appointment multiple times. Of course, many times, having to change is necessary or appropriate. Here are some good basic Netiquette rules to apply:

1. If it is not desired or necessary to have a meeting, session, or conversation (such as solicitation for a service), simply say no, and, if warranted, state clearly that the meeting is not desired.

2. Also provide a time frame in keeping with the circumstances. Be specific, whether the time frame is never, in a week, or longer. If possible, schedule the meeting or event immediately. If this is not possible, specify when the next contact should be and who should initiate it. If these details are left without a resolution or commitment, it is likely that confusion or unnecessary actions will result in time being wasted.

3. If an appointment needs to be moved, notify the appropriate parties. Good Netiquette behavior requires a brief apology and explanation. Usually it is not necessary to elaborate upon what specifics are involved.

4. Know the difference between postponing and canceling. Many people do not clearly specify if an event or meeting is meant to be postponed or, rather, canceled altogether. Either way, an explanation and regrets should be stated.

5. Confirmations: When an invitation is sent out or offered, request a reasonably prompt reply. If the process is automated, reply as quickly as possible. Should a tentative acceptance be necessary,

state when a definitive response will be provided. When an invitation has been proffered and no reasonable answer given, it is well within Netiquette guidelines to resend the request after a period of at least twenty-four hours. When initiating a second request, do so in a polite manner, without assumptions or scolding. Rather than feeling ignored, it may very well be the case that you have been the reason for the delay by virtue of a misspelling, wrongly selected email account, or aggressive spam filter. Regardless, it should never be assumed an invitee has received the request, opened it, or had the time to read it.

6. Reminders: The longer the time between an invitation and an event, the easier it is to have any lapses in attending. It is appropriate Netiquette to make sure that at least one reminder is sent between twenty-four and forty-eight hours of the scheduled event. If any of the attendees are traveling, make sure all are aware of this so as not to cancel or postpone without good reason. If the sender has sent at least one reminder and not had a confirmation, it is prudent either to call or send another polite message notifying the party or parties that without a reply, the meeting will need to be postponed (not canceled).

Scheduling group sessions

More and more companies are using group conferencing software over the Internet. These virtual meetings can involve anywhere from two people to hundreds or more. Similarly, they may be local or global in reach. Because of this, an invitation should be distinctively clear. Time zones must be considered and any changes minimized. The sample below reflects all of the information that should be given in the email. One should split an invitation with a calendar date and the dial-in number/URL. Every effort should be made to provide contact information in case of a technical issue or a need to communicate immediately before or during a meeting or online session. As mentioned previously, always include full date, day of the week, and time. Be mindful of possible religious holidays. Specify a minimum time slot, and leave open some optional time at the end of the requested time to address additional items which may arise during the discussion

Sample:

From: Mary Karl [mailto:messenger@webex.com]

Sent: Friday, May 25, 2012 3:43 p.m.

To: paul@tabularosa.net

Subject: Meeting invitation: XYZ Demonstration

Hello,

Mary Karl invites you to attend this online meeting.

Topic: XYZ Demonstration
Date: Friday, June 1, 2012
Time: 11:00 a.m., Eastern Daylight Time (New York, GMT-04:00)
Meeting Number: 123 555 9111
Meeting Password: PAUL0070

To join the online meeting (Now from mobile devices!)
----

1. Go to https://xyz.webex.com/xyz/j.php?ED=194933272&UID=1432845367&PW=NZGViNmQw
M2M2&RT=MiMxMQ%3D%3D
2. If requested, enter your name and email address.
3. If a password is required, enter the meeting password: PAUL0070
4. Click "Join".

To view in other time zones or languages, please click the link:

https://xyz.webex.com/xyz/j.php?ED=194933272&UID=1432845367&PW=NZGViNmQwM2M2&O
RT=MiMxMQ%3D%3D

To join the teleconference only

Call-in toll-free number: 1-(866) 700-5555 (US/Canada)

Show global numbers: https://www.tcconline.com/offSite/OffSiteController.jpf?cc=3400550

Conference Code: 340 055 0

For assistance

----

1. Go to https://xyz.webex.com/xyz/mc
2. On the left navigation bar, click "Support".

You can contact me at:
mkarl@xyz.com
123 5551212 Office
123 5551234 Cell

To add this meeting to your calendar program (for example, Microsoft Outlook), click this link:
https://xyz.webex.com/xyz/j.php?ED=194933272&UID=1432845367&ICS=MI&LD=1&RD=2&ST=1&SHA2=xyssIMhSd8rcjgncQ1i4-z7m4-tMvBBYNzw5alyDDNc=&RT=MiMxMQ%3D%3D

The playback of UCF (Universal Communications Format) rich media files requires appropriate players. To view this type of rich media files in the meeting, please check whether you have the players installed on your computer by going to https://xyz.webex.com/xyz/systemdiagnosis.php.

Email follow-up to meetings

Proper Netiquette should be to follow up a session or meeting with a thank-you note. All questions should be answered. The same guidelines for a well-composed email should be followed. All specific actions for any commitments are important to define. Include all attendees or persons of interest in all communications.

Request or requirements for accepting/declining invitations

Any meeting, overt request, or notification has specific reasons for taking place. There are multitudes of considerations, degrees of importance, and reasons for the gathering. Based upon an event or meeting characteristics, there are various measure of Netiquette to maintain. The following are meeting definitions and Netiquette rules and specifications to consider. Some of these categories may be as follows:

1. Required

2. Optional

3. Closed

4. Open

Automated invitations

There are a number of products that automate meeting invitations. These products also provide the capability to include attachments, messages, or other information. The products also have requests for providing acceptance, refusal, or deferment. Netiquette considerations should be practiced as though these are regular emails.

When to send email invitations

The best times to send emails, in particular email invitations, are not likely to ever be universally agreed upon. Many people will agree that Tuesday and Thursday mornings between 7:30 a.m. and 8:30 a.m. are best. These times are likely to have the least amount of backed up correspondences. Additionally, reaching "early birds" at their computers is likelier. Finally, these times will have fewer meetings, appointments, or events started. If someone is en route to work or the office, he or she may see arriving email via phone.

If previous communications exist, one can make note as to when a responder has sent replies. The best procedure is to schedule these times to the sender with calendar reminders or software schedulers. For example, if a recipient has sent emails during evening hours, this would be prime time for attempting to connect. There are some users who are often online at work, late, early, weekends, and even holidays.

Responding to email invitations

There are many important Netiquette basics to maintain in a reply to an email invitation. It should be emphasized that a prompt response is tantamount when replying to such an email, in particular when there are multiple attendees.

Some useful Netiquette tips

1. If an offline meeting has been scheduled, it is best to follow up with an immediate email. Requesting a confirmation is a necessity.

2. The inviter should send a confirmation email the day before an appointment. If the appointment is in two weeks or more, a reminder should be sent every seven to ten business days.

3. If a meeting attendee is required to travel, this should be stated in a confirmation email with a cutoff date/time for cancellation.

4. Confirmations should include the specifics of a meeting, not just a plain statement.

5. Provide reasonable lead time in scheduling appointments, particularly for those with multiple attendees.

6. Focus the time, date, and location to best accommodate everyone required to be there, or those who typically have less available time.

7. If an appointment has high importance for any of the attendees, it is essential to state this clearly in all of the correspondence.

8. If travel expense or extended effort is necessary, a cancellation deadline should be politely stated.

9. In current times with fewer meetings occurring, it is financially important that all details and items be thoroughly and explicitly clear.

10. Specify all items attendees should or are expected to bring.

11. Items to show in all email appointments include the following:

    A. Location with street address, floor, and room number

    B. Time (identify time zone) with day of the week, date

    C. Expected duration with hard stop times, if any

    D. Directions, maps, or how to get them

    E. Dress code

    F. Accessibility, parking

    G. Location accessibility, including alternate phone numbers

12. Send reminder messages. Include date and time in the subject field. Get to the point and provide a means of contact, similar to what one would do when making an appointment.

Forwarding invitations

Considerable care and thought should always be given to forwarding invitations. Core etiquette and Netiquette principles maintain almost sacrosanct adherence to avoid misusing the privacy of communications. If a situation is presented where an invitee wishes to add someone to a private meeting, social event, or other gathering, there are a number of steps that should be taken:

1. Seek permission of the inviter (original sender).

2. Determine who should be on the distribution list.

3. Copy the original invitee.

4. Remove unnecessary threads, but keep confidentiality clauses and disclaimers.

5. Identify that this is a forwarded document.

6. Ask the recipient not to forward the document, or attach a legal notice, if necessary.

7. Never assume a sender will approve of forwarding correspondence.

8. Do not forward documents if under nondisclosure or confidentiality agreements.

9. Never add controversial, discriminatory, or derogatory comments to the basic text.

10. Explain briefly and clearly to the recipient why the invitation is being forwarded. One should be mindful that some people will be offended because they were not original invitees.

11. One may be selective in showing a full list of invitees, depending on any number of reasons, including size of the list, possible effect on attendance, specific instructions, or any number of other reasons.

Hello:

This meeting invitation is being forwarded to you with permission of (invitee). We both agreed you were inadvertently omitted from the initial list. Kindly excuse this oversight.

Sincerely

Paul J. Babicki
Tabula Rosa Systems
609 8181802 office
609 462 8031 cell
www.tabularosa.net

Postponements and cancellations

Seemingly, in this age of cyberspace, appointments are either postponed or canceled far more frequently than only a short time ago. As stated previously, the Netiquette distinction between a postponement and a cancellation is that a postponement is temporary and is occurring because of considerations that cause an attendee to be unavailable. A cancellation is an implicit and permanent or long-term action.

Typically, a postponement by email will include a requested re-scheduling date and time. If it is necessary to postpone a meeting or appointment, the message should make this known right away, both in the subject line and the first paragraph of the email. Additionally, a brief explanation is usually appropriate. Usually details need not be included unless they are pertinent to the attendees.

When canceling a meeting or appointment, the permanence of this should be made very clear. It is highly recommended, and best Netiquette, to give an explanation or reason. The details and depth are relevant to the importance of the meeting. Keep normal Netiquette basics in terms of consistency, tone, and content. Keep in mind the permanency of the cancellation for future considerations.

Replying to postponements and cancellations

After receiving a cancellation without a specific explanation given, it is certainly acceptable to request a reason. This should be done with full Netiquette. If a postponement with a rescheduled time has been received, it is best Netiquette not to ask for a reason if one is not given. Prompt confirmations should be provided for both rescheduling and canceled appointments.

Requesting confirmations

Every invitation should include a request for a confirmation. If an acknowledgment is not received within twenty-four to forty-eight hours before the scheduled session, an additional request should be submitted.

1. When one sends a postponement or cancellation, a confirmation should be asked for, particularly if there is travel expense or multiple people involved.

2. If a postponement alternative time is set, it is important to make sure this is clearly stated.

3. If a request to confirm is not answered after reasonable times and repeated messages, proper Netiquette allows for the meeting to be postponed or cancelled.

Conclusion

> **"Communication leads to community, that is, to understanding intimacy and mutual valuing."**
>
> - Rollo May

Most of this book has focused upon immediate ways to reduce common Netiquette errors. Although case-by-case corrections and adjustments are good, the fundamental issues of creating and sustaining Netiquette education, rules, conventions, and practices are virtually nonexistent. There is no indication of anything being done to improve upon this. Similarly, traditional English studies, including grammar, composition, and usage rules are diminishing.

It is a paradox that a communication form used by over one-third of the world's population has no published usage structure. It is an enigma that a technology so dynamic and driven has actually made most of its users less productive by not contributing to people's improvement in lucid communications. The rapidly growing global society and economy can only be better served by more useful, not more voluminous, communication. If the volume of communication cannot be reduced, then it is vital that communication be made better. Contrast the effects of Netiquette "health" with children's health. Allowing bad grammar daily is as though one is allowing children to eat high-fat food and sugar drinks morning, noon, and night. Bad habits can have the same impact on communication skills as early smoking can on life-long health.

Better, clearer email and electronic messaging can avert disasters, give millions access to critical information, and deliver news instantaneously. Misinformation over the millennia has sometimes contributed to or even caused conflicts. False, controlled information has sometimes contributed to atrocities, fanaticism, violence, and many other negative repercussions. What Netiquette at its best offers is a reduction of misunderstanding, tempered language, diplomacy, and a vehicle for consistency in written communication.

Communications should be enhanced and improved upon significantly as technology increases, offering many capabilities to facilitate development of programs and prompting education (such as online courses or eschools). Faster and clearer exchanges of information can reduce many social barriers, strengthen relationships, and promote exchanges of ideas. Additionally, misunderstandings, false information, and harmful rumors all can be remediated and alleviated by using rapid communication.

With all of the great benefits that arise with communication technology advancement, there are, conversely, many damaging situations and negative consequences. Some of the most obvious of these are malware, harassment, libel, privacy infringement, and social humiliation.

It is my hope that my work will provide a stepping-stone to awareness that technology's vast improvement in message communication will be accompanied by equivalent advancement in the effectiveness of its content. It is not implausible to assume that places of learning can offer courses, resources, and measurement to contribute to effective cyber language and Netiquette. Ideally, as effective email communications increase, there are so many positive ramifications that can occur both now and well into the future. If used properly, advancement in communication technology is directed to

> "In fine, I have written my work, not as an essay which is to win the applause of the moment, but as a possession for all time."
>
> - Thucydides

bringing about positive changes in our world. When people communicate properly, good and great things often happen. These positive outcomes might be resolving personal issues between two people, or they might be bringing together people to share a common cause.

Proper communications is the simplest and most profound method of achieving local, regional and global benefit. All segments of social, political, environmental and critical events can be understood and resolved. Netiquette practiced in its complete form offers all people from all demographics and cultures the capabilities of using the dynamics of technological advancement to achieve a betterment for all ... within periods of time unimaginable only a few years ago. Let us all work together to bring these dynamics to fulfillment.

References

1. "Internet 2012 in numbers," posted in *Tech blog* on January 16, 2013, http://www.royal.pingdom.com/2013/01/16/internet-2012-in-numbers/.

2. Kruger, Justin; Epley, Nicholas; Parker, Jason; Ng, Zhi-Wen, "Egocentrism over e-mail: Can we communicate as well as we think?" *Journal of Personality and Social Psychology*, Volume 89(6), December 2005, pp. 925-936.

3. Verhoeven, Daniel; "Can we resolve ambiguity by email? Comparing computer mediated communication with face-to-face communication in the real world," 2006.

   https://docs.google.com/viewer?a=v&q=cache:39G0h9qfrKEJ:ho me.deds.nl/~danielverhoeven/PDF/Can_We_Resolve_Ambiguity_by_Email.pdf+Daniel+Verhoeven,+can+we+resolve+ambiguity+by+email&hl=en&gl=us&pid=bl&srcid=ADGEESi1wCLqR gitOFt8iF62qe7HVWYG9KdK5SmRmfCT2f6FOa1ZGHOrRKg GbMQkGl23n0x0_4hL-KIlU5yZfQaSNLTgMIDcPspV0O4hHz-9PEKU1CMA3QrAf7l2l7m0XxTXyCGfXwsP1&sig=AHIEtbSoV udPYy4Etu0U3RbtkXdmmbETGw

4. Message Anti-Abuse Working Group, MAAWG, http://www.maawg.org

5. Enemark, Daniel, "It's all about me: Why e-mails are so easily misunderstood," *The Christian Science Monitor*, May 15, 2006.

6. Radicati, Sara, "Email statistics report, 2013-2017," *The Radicati Group, Inc.,* http://www.radicati.com.

7. Osterman, Michael, "Is email really going away?" published February 25, 2013, http://messagingnews.com/osterman.

8. Naquin, Charles E.; Kurtzberg, Terri R.; Belkin, Liuba Y., "The finer points of lying online: E-mail versus pen and paper." *Journal of Applied Psychology*, Vol 95(2), Mar 2010, pp. 387-394.

9. Karasaridis, Aliki, "Online censorship in 2012," http://mg.co.za/article/2012-11-20-looking-back-on-2012-online-censorship

10. The US Department of Homeland Security Analyst-Desktop-Binder 2011 (http://www.scribd.com/doc/82701103/Analyst-Desktop-Binder-REDACTED) pp. 20-23.

11. http://www.a-to-z-of-manners-and-etiquette.com/

12. http://www.dailywritingtips.com/strunk-and-whites-the-elements-of-style/

13. Grammar Slammer: http://englishplus.com/grammar/

14. The Purdue Online Writing Lab: http://owl.english.purdue.edu/

15. Acronym Finder: http://www.acronymfinder.com

16. The Gregg Reference Manual is for anyone who writes, edits, or prepares material for distribution or publication. http://www.mhhe.com/business/buscom/gregg/

17. The blue book of grammar and punctuation: http://www.grammarbook.com/

18. http://www.spellcheck.net/

19. http://www.merriam-webster.com/

20. Internet slang dictionary and translator: http://www.noslang.com/

21. "16 Rules for Writing Numbers" http://www.slideshare.net/Caroynl/16-rules-for-writing-numbers#btnNext

Appendix A - Powerful and Beautiful Words

abundance/abundant
accomplished
accuracy
adaptability
admirable
adroit
affirmative
agile
attainable
auspicious
balanced
brilliance
clarity
coalesce
compelling
confidence
conflate
consistent
cornerstone
creative
dazzling
decisive
dedicated
devoted
dexterous

earnest
effervescent
elegant
encompass
enduring
energy
envision
epiphany
epitome
equilibrium
esteemed
etiquette
evocative
exuberant
faithful
far-reaching
felicity
flexible
fluidity
generous
genuine
graceful
gracious
harmonious
imbue

independence

innovative

iridescent

judicious

laudatory

lithe

loyalty

magnificent

meaningful

melodious

perceptive

plentiful

praiseworthy

precision

proven

purity

quality

quintessential

reliable

resilience

resonant

resounding

sound

stalwart

surpass

tasteful

transcend

transformative

unfailing

worthiness

zenith

Appendix B - Irritating Phrases

The most irritating phrases:

1. At the end of the day
2. Quite frankly
3. I personally
4. At this moment in time
5. With all due respect
6. Absolutely
7. It's a nightmare
8. Shouldn't of
9. 24/7
10. It's not rocket science
11. Very unique
12. It's not brain surgery (related to number 10)
13. Perfect (related to number 6)
14. No problem
15. For sure
16. FYI
17. ASAP
18. To tell the truth
19. You have caught me away
20. No way
21. Out of the box
22. Ergonomically
23. My bad
24. Not to worry
25. No worries
26. In my humble opinion (IMHO)
27. Dude!
28. Swell
29. Right on!
30. Yeah
31. Pursuant
32. As per our discussion
33. Totally
34. Should of
35. At the risk of being repetitive
36. KISS (Keep it simple, stupid)
37. Hit (visit)
38. Distro (Distribution list)
39. Bang for the buck
40. Viral
41. That type of thing
42. Epic fail
43. I'm just saying
44. Chat

45. No brainer
46. Slam dunk
47. You betcha
48. Seriously
49. To make a long story short
50. To be perfectly honest
51. Truth of the matter
52. I am sure you will agree
53. Take it to the next level
54. The thing is

55. As it were
56. And so forth
57. Mark my words
58. Bring it on
59. Works for me
60. You know
61. I am not going to lie
62. For all intents and purposes
63. Team player
64. Quick learner

Appendix C - Writing Numbers

1. If a number begins a sentence, it should be written out.

Example: Twelve people won an award for helping with the auction.

2. Spell out single-digit whole numbers. Use figures for numbers greater than ten.

Correct: I want two pencils.

I want 11 pencils.

3. Categories should be written with consistency. For instance, if you choose numerals because one of the numbers is greater than ten, use numerals for all numbers in that category. If you choose to spell out numbers because one of the numbers is a single digit, spell out all numbers in that category.

Correct: All 15 students from my class joined in with 3 students from the other class to make the homecoming banner.

All fifteen students from my class joined in with three students from the other class to make the homecoming banner.

The budget accommodates 18 trees to be purchased for the three parking islands and 6 trees to be bought for the two walkways. (Trees are represented with figures; locations are represented with words.)

Incorrect: I asked for six apples, not 60.

4.	Always spell out simple fractions and use hyphens with them.
Examples:	One-half of the cookies have been eaten.
	A two-thirds majority is required to pass the motion.
5.	Write mixed fractions in figures unless it is the first word of a sentence.
Examples:	We expect a 3 1/2 percent price increase.
	Three and one-half percent was the maximum allowable penalty.
6.	Round large numbers are usually spelled out. Be careful to be consistent within a sentence. Use figures, even with numbers less than 11 and for numbers of technical significance including money, percentages, pages, sizes, measurements, clock time, coordinates, and so forth.
Correct:	You can earn from two thousand to five thousand dollars.
Incorrect:	You can earn from two thousand to $5,000.
Correct:	You can earn from six hundred to seven million dollars.
	You can earn from $6 hundred to $7 million.
Incorrect:	You can earn from $600 to $7 million.
	You can earn from $600 to seven million dollars.
7.	Write decimals in figures. Put a zero in front of a decimal unless the decimal itself begins with a zero.
Examples:	The river rose 0.89 of a foot in one rainfall.
	The river rose only .04 of a foot this year because of the drought.

8.	When numbers have decimal points, use a comma only when the number has five or more digits before the decimal point. Position the comma in front of the third digit to the left of the decimal point. Use a comma where it would appear in the figure format. Include the word *and* where the decimal point appears in the figure format.
Examples:	$12,879.21: Twelve thousand, eight hundred seventy-nine dollars and twenty-one cents
	$2435: Two thousand four hundred thirty-five dollars
	Note: If the number has no decimal point, experts disagree on whether to begin using the comma with four-digit numbers or to begin using the comma with five-digit numbers. When writing out these numbers, use the comma where it appears in the numerical form.
	2,011 students: two thousand, eleven students
9.	When writing dates, use figures and cardinal numbers (4,5,6), not ordinal (4th, 5th, 6th) numbers.
Examples:	The February 8 meeting has been cancelled.
	On November 21, 2012 he opened his bank account.
10.	When describing decades, they should be spelled out and in lowercase.
Example:	During the fifties and sixties, rock and roll music became popular.
11.	Refer to decades in the following formats. Put an apostrophe (not an opening quotation mark, as automatically placed by some word processing programs) before the incomplete number but not between the year and the *s*.
Correct:	During the late ′50s and throughout the ′60s, rock and roll music became popular in the US.

Incorrect:	During the late '50's and throughout the '60's, rock and roll music became popular in the US.
12.	Decades can be described as complete numerals. Again, there is no apostrophe between the year and the *s*.
Example:	During the 1950s and 1960s, rock and roll music increased in popularity.
13.	Spell out the time of day in text, even with half and quarter hours. Additionally, when using *o'clock*, the number is always spelled out.
Examples:	He gets up at five thirty before the children wake up.
	The coffee is brewed at five o'clock in the morning.
14.	Use numerals for the time of day when exact times are being emphasized or when using a.m. or p.m.
Examples:	Her bus leaves at 7:15 a.m.
	Please arrive by 10:30 sharp.
	She had a 5 p.m. deadline.
15.	When writing a date that includes BC or AD, do not use a comma in numbers.
Correct:	1500 BC
Incorrect:	1,500 BC
16.	Refer to *noon* and *midnight*, not *12:00 p.m.* and *12:00 a.m.*
17.	Use hyphenation for numbers from twenty-one through ninety-nine.
Example:	Twenty-four people were injured in the plane crash.

Appendix D - SMTP Error Messages

The Meaning of the Numbers

All robust-email users encounter returned messages. When reading the reasons given for returns, a large percentage of the senders do not understand the explanations. The following list provides brief definitions for the most common email errors. These are important to reference from a Netiquette point of view, in case a late or resent message or unavoidable error happens to serve as a reason for issues such as missing deadlines or similar occurrences.

A mail server will reply to every request a client (such as your email program) makes with a return code. This code consists of three numbers.

The first number usually signifies whether the server accepted the command and if it could handle it. There are five possible values:

1. The server has accepted the command but does not yet take action. A confirmation message is required. Currently, this is not used.

2. The server has completed the task successfully.

3. The server has understood the request but requires further information to complete it.

4. The server has encountered a temporary failure.

5. The server has encountered an error.

The second number gives more information. These six errors are defined as follows:

- **0** A syntax error has occurred

- **1** Informational reply to a request

- **2** A referral to the connection status

- **3** and **4** are not generally used

- **5** References the status of the mail system and the mail server

The last number is the best recognized and shows more detail of the mail transfer status. The list names ESMTP server response codes, as defined in RFC 821 extensions.

- **211** - A system status message

- **214** - A help message for a human reader follows.

- **220** - SMTP service ready

- **221** - Service closing

- **250** - Requested action taken and completed

- **251** - The recipient is not local to the server, but the server will accept and forward the message.

- **252** - The recipient cannot be verified, but the server accepts the message and attempts delivery.

- **354** - Start message input and end with <CRLF>.<CRLF>. This indicates that the server is ready to accept the message itself (after you have told it who it is from and where you want it to go).

- **421** - The service is not available, and the connection will be closed.

- **450** - The requested command failed because the user's mailbox was unavailable—for example, because it was locked. Try again later.

- **451** - The command has been aborted due to a server error.

- **452** - The command has been aborted because the server has insufficient system storage.

The following error messages (500–504) are for the email client.

- **500** - The server could not recognize the command due to a syntax error.

- **501** - A syntax error was encountered in command arguments.

- **502** - This command is not implemented.

- **503** - The server has encountered a bad sequence of commands.

- **504** - A command parameter is not implemented.

- **550** - The user's mailbox was unavailable. Either it no longer exists, or the message was blocked for security or policy rules.

- **551** - The recipient is not local to the server.

- **552** - The action was aborted due to exceeded storage allocation.

- **553** - The command was aborted because the mailbox name is invalid.

- **554** - The transaction failed. There could be many reasons, such as an outage, software, or network failure.

Appendix E - Email Closings

Business email closings

- My sincere thanks for your consideration
- Sincerely
- Cordially
- Best regards/wishes for our mutual success
- Cheers (less formal)
- Kind regards/wishes
- Many thanks
- I remain yours truly
- Respectfully yours
- Warm regards
- Yours respectfully/sincerely/truly
- Very truly yours
- Most sincerely

Friendly email closings

- Good wishes
- Yours
- Greetings to all
- Kind thoughts

- Take care/take good care

- Wishing you the best

- Write soon

- Your friend

- Until next time

- Stay in touch

- Cheers

Informal only

- Stay tuned for more

- Stand by

- Be good/well

- Cheerio

- More to come

- Take care

- Take it easy

- Until next time

- See you soon

- Stay well

- So much for now

- Many more

- Adiós

- Aloha

- Your friend

- Health and happiness

Appendix F - Key Email and Internet Spellings

Presently, there are varying standards for spelling Internet words and terms. While many of the words listed below may be spelled with hyphens, the easiest way to remember is to use capital letters and hyphens as little as possible. I recommend the following:

- cybernet

- cyberspace

- cyberbullying

- ebook

- ebrary/elibrary

- ecard

- ecommerce

- ejournal

- elearning

- elottery

- email

- emusic

- epolicy

- epology (portmanteau: email apology)

- epublishing
- ereader
- eschool
- esign
- etrash
- evite
- ewallet
- ezine
- homepage
- inbox
- Internet (the entity is capitalized, as opposed to the term internetworking)
- intranet
- IP (uppercase)
- iPad
- mailbox
- Netiquette (portmanteau)
- offline
- online
- outbox
- URL
- vcard
- Web
- WebEx (when the service is used; *webex*, generic)

- webinar

- webmaster

- webpage

- website

- WiFi

- www

Appendix G - United States Domain-Name File Extensions

.aero	Aviation
.biz	Business organizations
.com	Commercial
.coop	Cooperative organizations
.edu	Educational
.gov	US Government
.info	Open TLD (Top Level Domain)
.int	(usually NATO)
.jobs	Used by human resources departments to list and promote job listings
.mil	US Department of Defense
.mobi	Mobile devices
.museum	Museums
.name	Personal
.net	Networks
.org	Organizations
.travel	Traveling

Appendix H - List of File Extensions

File extensions are based on using all possible combinations of English characters. Three alpha characters show a possible combination of close to twenty thousand possibilities. If numbers or additional letters are added, far more combinations are possible. There are a number of categories for file extensions. Among these are compression data archive, media archiving, computer-aided design, database, fonts, graphs (vector, 3D), object code, source code, and music. There are more categories for scientific, video, games, medical, and more. The following list shows most of the formats used in common email.

3DS	3D Studio	ASC	ASCII file
8BF	Adobe Photoshop	ASCX	ASP.NET file
AAC	Advanced audio coding (Mac)	ASD	Word temporary document
APP	Apple executable	ASMX	ASP.NET file
AFM	Adobe font metrics (Type 1)	ASP	Active Server Page
AI	Adobe Illustrator graphics,	ASPX	ASP.NET file
AIF	Digital audio (Mac)	ATT	AT&T Group IV fax
AIFC	Digital audio (Mac)	AU	Digital audio (Sun)
AJAX	Asynchronous JavaScript And XML	AVI	Microsoft movie format
		BAK	Backup
ALB	JASC Image Commander	BAS	BASIC source code
ANI	Animated cursor	BAT	DOS, OS/2 batch file
ANN	Windows help annotations	BIN	Driver, overlay
ANS	ANSI text	BML	Bookmark library (SyncURL)
ARC	ARC, ARC+ compressed archive	BMP	Windows and OS/2 bitmap
ASA	ASP info	BMK	Windows help bookmarks
ASAX	ASP.NET file	C	C source code

CAB	Microsoft compressed format for distribution	DCA	IBM text
CAL	Windows calendar	DCM	DICOM medical image
CCB	Visual Basic animated button	DCS	Color separated EPS format
CDA	CD audio track	DCX	Intel fax image
CDX	FoxPro and Clipper index	DCT	Dictionary
CFG	Configuration	DEF	Definition
CGM	CGM vector graphics	DIB	Windows DIB bitmap
CHK	DOS/Windows corrupted file (Chkdsk)	DIC	Dictionary
		DIF	Spreadsheet
CIT	Intergraph scanned image	DISCO	Publishing and Discovering Web Services
COB	COBOL source code	DLG	Dialogue script
COB	Truespace 3D file	DLL	Dynamic link library
CLP	Windows clipboard	DOC	Microsoft Word Document (2003–2007)
CLS	Visual Basic class module		
CMP	JPEG bitmap, LEAD bitmap	DOCX	Microsoft Word Document (2008)
CMP	RichLink composed format		
CNT	Windows help contents	DOT	Microsoft Word template
COM	Executable program	DPI	Pointline bitmap
CPD	Fax cover document	DRV	Driver
CPE	Fax cover document	DWG	AutoCAD vector format
CPI	DOS code page	DX	Autotrol document imaging
CPL	Windows control panel applets	DXF	AutoCAD vector format
CPP	C++ source code	ED5	EDMICS bitmap (DOD)
CPR	Knowledge Access bitmap	EMF	Enhanced Windows metafile
CRD	Cardfile file	EPS	Encapsulated PostScript
CSV	Comma delimited	EXE	Executable program
CUR	Cursor	FAX	Various fax formats
CUT	Dr. Halo bitmap	FLC	Autodesk animation
CV5	Canvas 5 vector/bitmap	FLI	Autodesk animation
DAT	Data	FLT	Graphics conversion filter
DB	Paradox table	FMT	dBASE screen format
DBF	dBASE database	FMV	FrameMaker raster and vector graphics
DBT	dBASE text		

FNT	Windows font	IDD	MIDI instrument definition
FOG	Fontographer font	IDE	Development environment
FON	Windows bitmapped font		configuration
FON	Telephone file	IMG	Macintosh image file
FOR	FORTRAN source code	IMG	GEM Paint bitmap
FOT	Windows TrueType font infor-	INF	Setup information
	mation	INI	Initialization
FPX	FlashPix bitmap	JAR	JAVA data
FRM	dBASE report layout	JFF	JPEG bitmap
FTG	Windows Help-file links	JIF	JPEG bitmap
FTS	Windows Help-text search index	JPG	JPEG bitmap
GDF	GDDM format	JS	JavaScript file
GED	Arts and letters graphics	JT	JT Fax
GEM	GEM vector graphics	JTF	JPEG bitmap
GID	Windows help global index	KDC	Kodak Photo bitmap
GIF	CompuServe bitmap	KFX	Kofax Group IV fax
GP4	CALS Group IV—ITU Group IV	LBL	dBASE label
GRA	Microsoft graph	LEG	Legacy text
GRP	Windows ProgMan Group	LIB	Function library
GZ	UNIX Gzip	LIT	Microsoft Reader file
H	C header	LOG	Log file
HED	HighEdit document	LQT	Liquid Audio
HGL	HP Graphics language	LSN	Topic list (CDE)
HLP	Help text	LST	List
HPJ	Visual Basic help project	LV	LaserView Group IV
HPP	C++ program header	M1V	MPEG file
HPL	HP graphics language	M3U	MPEG file
HT	HyperTerminal	MAC	MacPaint bitmap
HTM	HTML document (web page)	MAK	Visual Basic/MS C++ project
HTML	HTML document (web page)	MAP	Link editor map
HTX	HTML extension file	MBX	Mailbox (email)
ICA	IBM MO:DCA - IOCA bitmap	MCS	MathCAD format
ICO	Windows icon	MCW	Word for Macintosh document
IDC	Internet database connector	MDB	Access database

MDF	Microsoft SQL server database	OBZ	Microsoft Office wizard
MET	OS/2 Metafile	OEB	Open eBook publication
MEU	Menu items	OPF	Open package file
MDX	dBASE IV multi-index	ORG	Organizer file
MID	MIDI sound file	OTF	OpenType font
MME	MIME-encoded file	OVL	Overlay module
MMF	Microsoft mail file	OVR	Overlay module
MMM	Macromind animation format	OUT	Encyclopedia definitions
MOD	Eudora script file	P10	Tektronix Plot 10
MOV	QuickTime movie	PAL	Windows palette
MPA	MPEG file	PAS	Pascal source code
MP2	MPEG file	PBD	PowerBuilder dynamic library
MP2V	MPEG file	PBK	Microsoft Phonebook
MP3	MPEG-1 Layer 3 audio	PBM	Portable Bitmap
MPE	MPEG file	PCL	HP LaserJet series
MPEG	MPEG file	PCD	Photo CD bitmap
MPG	MPEG file	PCM	LaserJet cartridge information
MPP	Microsoft Project	PCS	PICS animation
MSG	Message file	PCT	PC Paint bitmap
MSP	Microsoft Paint bitmap	PCT	Macintosh PICT bitmap and vector graphics
MUS	Music		
MVB	Microsoft Multimedia Viewer	PCW	PC Write document
MYD	MYSQL table data	PCX	PC Paintbrush bitmap
MYI	MYSAM table index	PDF	Portable Document Format (Acrobat),
M1V	MPEG file		
NAP	NAPLPS format	PDV	PC Paintbrush printer driver
NDX	dBASE index	PFA	Type 1 font (ASCII)
NDX	CDE index	PFB	Type 1 font
NG	Norton Guides text	PFM	Windows Type 1 font metrics
NLM	NetWare NLM program	PIC	Vector formats
O	UNIX machine language	PIC	Mac PICT format
OAZ	OAZ Fax	PIC	IBM Storyboard bitmap
OBD	Microsoft Office binder	PIF	Windows info. for DOS programs
OBJ	Machine language		
OBJ	Wavefront 3D file	PIF	IBM Picture Interchange

PL	Perl script	RM	Real Media file
PLT	AutoCAD plotter file	RMI	MIDI music
PLT	HPGL plotter file	RMM	Real Media file
PNG	PNG bitmap	RNL	GTX Run length bitmap
POV	POV-Ray ray tracing	RTF	Rich-text format (Microsoft)
PPD	PostScript printer description	RV	Real Video file
PPM	Portable Pixel map	SAT	ACIS 3-D model
PPS	PowerPoint Slideshow	SAV	Saved file
PPT	PowerPoint	SBP	IBM Storyboard graphics/Superbase text
PRD	Microsoft Word printer driver		
PRG	dBASE source code	SC2	Microsoft Schedule+ 7
PRN	Temporary print file	SCD	Microsoft Schedule+ 7
PRT	Formatted text	SCH	Microsoft Schedule+ 1
PS	PostScript page description	SCM	ScreenCam movie
PSD	Photoshop native format	SCP	Dial-up Networking script
PST	Microsoft Outlook file	SCR	Windows screen saver
PUB	Microsoft Publisher publication	SCR	Fax image
PUZ	Crossword puzzle	SCR	dBASE screen layout
PVK	Private Key	SET	Setup parameters
PWL	Windows password list	SLD	AutoCAD slide
QBW	QuickBooks	SND	Digital audio
QLB	Quick programming library	SWF	Shockwave file
QT	QuickTime movie	SYS	DOS, OS/2 driver
QTM	QuickTime movie	TAL	Adobe Type Align shaped text
RA	Real Audio file	TAR	Tape archive
RAM	Real Audio file	TAX	TurboTax
RAS	Sun bitmap	TAZ	UNIX Gzip archive
RAW	3D file (open standard)	TGZ	UNIX Gzip archive
RC	Resource script	TIF	TIFF bitmap
REC	Recorder file	TLB	OLE type library
REG	Registration file	TMP	Temporary
RFT	DCA/RFT document	TOC	Table of contents
RIA	Alpharel Group IV bitmap	TRM	Terminal file
RLE	Compressed	TTC	TrueType font compressed

TTF	TrueType font	WSH	Windows Scrip Host properties
TXT	ASCII text	WVL	Wavelet compressed file
VCF	vCard file	WVX	WMV metafile (location of
VOC	Sound Blaster sound		WMV file)
VOX	Voxware compressed audio	XBM	X Window bitmap
VSD	Visio drawing	XFX	JetFax
VUE	dBASE relational view	XLA	Excel add-in
WAV	Digital Audio (Windows)	XLB	Excel toolbar
WAX	WMA metafile (location of	XLC	Excel chart
	WMA file)	XLD	Excel dialogue
WBK	Microsoft Word backup	XLK	Excel backup
WBT	WinBatch file	XLM	Excel macro
WDB	Microsoft works data file	XLS	Excel spreadsheet
WIF	Wavelet image	XLT	Excel template
WIZ	Microsoft Word wizard	XLW	Excel project
WMA	Windows Media Audio (ASF	XML	XML file
	file)	XPM	X Window pixel map
WMF	Windows Metafile	XSD	XML schema
WMV	Windows Media video (ASF file)	XWD	X Window dump
WPS	Microsoft Works document	Z	UNIX Gzip archive
WRI	Windows Write document	ZIP	PKZIP compressed
WRL	VRML page	$$$	Temporary

Appendix I - Cardinal Rules of Netiquette

1. Never criticize others.

2. Honor commitments made in writing.

3. Be consistent in tone, content, and process.

4. Always maintain civility and politeness.

5. Apologize for and forgive harmless mistakes quickly without prejudice.

6. Always know and practice that Netiquette is more than manners. It also rests on a foundation of veracity, character, and ethics.

7. Do not take immediate exception to full factual knowledge.

8. Do not assume situations.

9. Never use bad language.

10. Be consistent with all positive practices of Netiquette.

Appendix J - Top Ten Types of Spam

1. Adult dating
2. Anti-spam
3. Insurance
4. Auto
5. Personal finance
6. Information technology
7. Diet and health
8. Travel
9. Educational
10. Political

Appendix K - Homeland Security Words to Avoid

Domestic Security

Assassination
Attack
Domestic security
Drill
Exercise
Cops
Law enforcement
Authorities
Disaster assistance
Disaster management
DNDO (Domestic Nuclear Detection Office)
National preparedness
Mitigation
Prevention
Response
Recovery
Dirty bomb
Domestic nuclear detection

Emergency management
Emergency response
First responder
Homeland security
Maritime domain awareness (MDA)
National preparedness initiative
Militia
Shooting
Shots fired
Evacuation
Deaths
Hostage
Explosion (explosive)
Police
Disaster medical assistance team (DMAT)
Organized crime

Gangs
National security
State of emergency
Security
Breach
Threat
Standoff
SWAT
Screening
Lockdown
Bomb (squad or threat)
Crash
Looting
Riot
Emergency Landing
Pipe bomb
Incident
Facility

HAZMAT & Nuclear

Hazmat
Nuclear
Chemical spill
Suspicious package/device
Toxic
National laboratory
Nuclear facility
Nuclear threat
Cloud
Plume
Radiation
Radioactive

Leak
Biological infection (or event)
Chemical
Chemical burn
Biological
Epidemic
Hazardous
Hazardous material incident
Industrial spill
Infection
Powder (white)

Gas
Spillover
Anthrax
Blister agent
Chemical agent
Exposure
Burn
Nerve agent
Ricin
Sarin
North Korea

Health Concern + H1N1

Outbreak
Contamination
Exposure
Virus
Evacuation
Bacteria
Recall
Ebola
Food Poisoning
Foot and Mouth (FMD)
H5N1
Avian
Flu

Salmonella
Small Pox
Plague
Human to human
Human to Animal
Influenza
Center for Disease Control (CDC)
Drug Administration (FDA)
Public Health
Toxic
Agro Terror
Tuberculosis (TB)

Agriculture
Listeria
Symptoms
Mutation
Resistant
Antiviral
Wave
Pandemic
Infection
Water/air borne
Sick
Swine
Pork

Strain
Quarantine
H1N1
Vaccine

Tamiflu
Norvo Virus
Epidemic

World Health Organization
(WHO) (and components)
Viral Hemorrhagic Fever
E. Coli

Infrastructure Security
Infrastructure security
Airport
CIKR (Critical Infrastructure
& Key Resources)
AMTRAK
Collapse
Computer infrastructure
Communications
infrastructure
Telecommunications
Critical infrastructure
National infrastructure
Metro
WMATA

Airplane (and derivatives)
Chemical fire
Subway
BART
MARTA
Port Authority
NBIC (National
Biosurveillance Integration
Center)
Transportation security
Grid
Power
Smart
Body scanner

Electric
Failure or outage
Black out
Brown out
Port
Dock
Bridge
Cancelled
Delays
Service disruption
Power lines

Southwest Border Violence
Drug cartel
Violence
Gang
Drug
Narcotics
Cocaine
Marijuana
Heroin
Border
Mexico
Cartel
Southwest
Juarez
Sinaloa
Tijuana
Torreon
Yuma
Tucson
Decapitated
U.S. Consulate
Consular
El Paso

Fort Hancock
San Diego
Ciudad Juarez
Nogales
Sonora
Colombia
Mara salvatrucha
MS13 or MS-13
Drug war
Mexican army
Methamphetamine
Cartel de Golfo
Gulf Cartel
La Familia
Reynosa
Nuevo Leon
Narcos
Narco banners (Spanish
equivalents)
Los Zetas
Shootout
Execution

Gunfight
Trafficking
Kidnap
Calderon
Reyosa
Bust
Tamaulipas
Meth Lab
Drug trade
Illegal immigrants
Smuggling (smugglers)
Matamoros
Michoacana
Guzman
Arellano-Felix
Beltran-Leyva
Barrio Azteca
Artistic Assassins
Mexicles
New Federation

Terrorism

Terrorism	IED (Improvised Explosive	Suspicious substance
Al Qaeda (all spellings)	Device)	AQAP (AL Qaeda Arabian
Terror	Abu Sayyaf	Peninsula)
Attack	Hamas	AQIM (Al Qaeda in the
Iraq	FARC (Armed Revolutionary	Islamic Maghreb)
Afghanistan	Forces Colombia)	TTP (Tehrik-i-Taliban
Iran	IRA (Irish Republican Army)	Pakistan)
Pakistan	ETA (Euskadi ta Askatasuna)	Yemen
Agro	Basque Separatists	Pirates
Environmental terrorist	Hezbollah	Extremism
Eco terrorism	Tamil Tigers	Somalia
Conventional weapon	PLF (Palestine Liberation	Nigeria
Target	Front)	Radicals
Weapons grade	PLO (Palestine Liberation	Al-Shabaab
Dirty bomb	Organization	Home grown
Enriched	Car bomb	Plot
Nuclear	Jihad	Nationalist
Chemical weapon	Taliban	Recruitment
Biological weapon	Weapons cache	Fundamentalism
Ammonium nitrate	Suicide bomber	Islamist
Improvised explosive device	Suicide attack	

Weather/Disaster/Emergency

Emergency	Ice	Mud slide or Mudslide
Hurricane	Stranded/Stuck	Erosion
Tornado	Help	Power outage
Twister	Hail	Brown out
Tsunami	Wildfire	Warning
Earthquake	Tsunami Warning Center	Watch
Tremor	Magnitude	Lightening
Flood	Avalanche	Aid
Storm	Typhoon	Relief
Crest	Shelter-in-place	Closure
Temblor	Disaster	Interstate
Extreme weather	Snow	Burst
Forest fire	Blizzard	Emergency Broadcast System
Brush fire	Sleet	

Cyber Security

Cyber security	2600	Hacker
Botnet	Spammer	China
DDOS (dedicated denial of	Phishing	Conficker
service)	Rootkit	Worm
Denial of service	Phreaking	Scammers
Malware	Cain and abel	Social media
Virus	Brute forcing	
Trojan	Mysql injection	
Keylogger	Cyber attack	
Cyber Command	Cyber terror	

Source:

The US Department of Homeland Security Analyst-Desktop-Binder 2011 (http://www.scribd.com/doc/82701103/Analyst-Desktop-Binder-REDACTED)

Appendix L - Hackers' List of Worst Email Passwords

1. password

2. 123456

3. 12345678

4. qwerty

5. abc123

6. monkey

7. 1234567

8. letmein

9. trustno1

10. dragon

11. baseball

12. 111111

13. iloveyou

14. master

15. sunshine

16. ashley

17. bailey

18. passw0rd

19. shadow

20. 123123

21. 654321

22. superman

23. qazwsx

24. michael

25. football

Appendix M - Common abbreviations

1. c or ©   Copyright (©2013)

2. c. ca   "About," "around," circa; used with dates (*He was born c. 2000.*)

3. cf.   Compare or consult—used to provide contrasting or opposing information

4. ed.   Editor, edited, edition

5. e.g.   "For example," the abbreviation for *exempli gratia*

6. et al.   "And others," the abbreviation for *et alia*; also, elsewhere, the abbreviation for *et alibi*

7. etc.   "And so on" or "and so forth," the abbreviation for *et cetera*

8. ibid.   Abbreviation for *ibidem,* used in citations to refer again to the last source previously referenced

9. i.e.   "That is," the abbreviation for *id est*; used to give specific clarification via a restatement; "in other words"

10. loc. cit   "In the place cited"; used the same way as ibid.

11. ms. mss   Manuscript, manuscripts

12.	NB	"Note well," the abbreviation for *nota bene*
13.	nd	"No date;" used when the publication or copyright date of a source is not known
14.	op. cit	In the works cited; used the same as *ibid.* and *loc. cit*
15.	q.v.	"Which see," "whom see"; indicates that the reference is within the same source; encyclopedias may use this to refer to other entries within that same encyclopedia.
16.	viz.	"namely"
17.	vs.	"versus"

Made in the USA
Charleston, SC
06 March 2014